LI
AFTER
DEATH

ANSWERS AND NEW INSIGHTS

Dr Stephen Treloar

Life After Death

— OUR JOURNEY CONTINUES... —

Life After Death
— OUR JOURNEY CONTINUES... —

A Life After Death Publication

This paperback Australian edition was published in 2023.

ISBN 9798397108515

Part of every dollar spent on purchasing this book (or eBook version) is donated to the mission of the International Committee of the Red Cross (ICRC) to protect and assist victims and promote understanding and respect for international humanitarian law. Donations are made quarterly.

Life After Death

— OUR JOURNEY CONTINUES... —

Dedication

This book is dedicated to my wife Karen and grandchildren Leo John and River John, who bring enormous joy.

Also devoted to Jack Fay, my 94-year-old father-in-law who, at the tender age of five, survived his near-death experience : on 'leaving' his body and from high in the sky mistakenly noticed two rescuers kneeling over what he thought was his older 'brother' performing resuscitation. It was Jack himself, the one being resuscitated and brought back to life after 'drowning' in an area known locally as "Tent City" at Clontarf Beach, Sydney, in 1932. Jack went on to marry and fathered eight children but has never forgotten the day his 'brother' almost died. Jack is still active and living on the Mid-North Coast of New South Wales.

Dr. Stephen Treloar

Table Of Contents

Foreword

If you are seeking answers to perennial questions that have been asked through the ages, concerning the nature of the afterlife, death and dying, the permanence of the Soul, the 'state' and 'location' of heaven, hell, and the like - read this book !

In "Life After Death," Stephen provides a thoroughly researched, non-biased, and unfiltered overview of these topics from a philosophical and theological perspective, using language and academic style accessible to all readers, enabling them to form informed views and create questions for their continued reflection.

As a former Monk with interests in emotional intelligence, leadership, mindfulness, and spirituality, I found the thoughts and ideas expressed in this book of significant interest, many of which I had yet to consider.

In a science-driven world, where control and certainty are preferred and sought without having to navigate the terrain of ambiguity, uncertainty, and vulnerability, this book invites a step back to reconsider what has been accepted as fundamental truths that may not be as first understood.

This book gives the reader a deeper insight into negotiating a sympathetic understanding of the varied religious views 'out there.'

Socrates, the father of philosophy, says an unexamined life is not worth living. This excellent, well-researched, and superbly written book "Life After Death" lays the seed that enables examination of these perennial questions. I commend this book to you.

Jude-Martin Etuka, BA (Oxford), MA (Oxford), PhD (candidate), UNDA.

Disclaimer

The author and publisher have tried to provide researched information honestly and in good faith with the sources shown. In the event of attributing, missing, or incorrectly citing a reference, we unreservedly apologize ; if you email us, we will correct it in the next edition. The author also acknowledges and credits the use of AI in searching and retrieving information to provide various views and opinions, alongside citations from academics and news in the public domain. The subject areas covered in this book can be controversial, and some readers may be offended by what they read, particularly as it may challenge long-held beliefs. If this occurs, the author apologizes for any hurt and discomfort. Sometimes discovering the 'truth' is like fossicking for gold; you don't find what's genuine in gold-panning without some agitation.

Preface By Author

This book presents the findings of the author's five decades of searching, exploring, and researching life's great mysteries. Although the author is a former university academic and researcher with expertise in different subject areas, he seeks to reconcile theology with religious teachings, beliefs, and dogma against his observations and experiences.

The author explores several facets of "life after death" and questions such as "What happens when you die ?" "Is there a Heaven and Hell ?" and "Is communication possible ?" Although the author does not claim to have all the answers and is not a religious scholar, he delves into these topics with curiosity and an open mind.

The invaluable contribution of scientific study has undeniably expanded our understanding of the natural world, including Earth and space. It has provided medical expertise, experience, and advances in many other disciplines. However, applying the scientific method to "prove" or "disprove" areas of belief systems, theology, or religion is invalid. While science can use objectivity to identify the legitimacy of certain concepts, there are limitations to what science can reveal. It is important to note that just because science cannot necessarily prove something, it does not mean that it cannot be true.

For example, let us consider the existence of God. As of 2010, reports from Statista.com indicate that 45% of the world's population believes in God (or a supreme being). The highest number of believers is reported at 93% in Indonesia; 56% in India; 50% in Italy; 46% in Canada; 29% in Australia; 25% in Great Britain; 9% in China, and 4% in Japan. The question of the existence of God is subjective and difficult to be measured by the scientific method; moreover, if the presence of God became a proven scientific fact, it would be arguably counterproductive to God's plan — it would remove the essential ingredient of "faith" and undermine the gift of 'free will.'

The study of life beyond death is an exciting area of research; the more you discover, or that which is revealed, creates new questions. The author shares the view that there is life after death. This revelation comforts those experiencing grief, either from losing a loved one or learning about the terminal health condition of a loved one or oneself.

Whether you find yourself nodding in agreement or shaking your head in disagreement, something can be gained from the book's exploration of life after death. The book seeks to stimulate and encourage reflections outside the constrictions of religious dogma, catechism, and teaching. It can spark new thoughts and reflections on a topic that has fascinated humans for centuries, which can only be positive.

One of the fascinating aspects of belief in the afterlife is that it transcends religious boundaries. Nearly all religions support the fundamental view of "life" beyond mortal means. With so many religions presenting their own "truth" through their interpretative lens, they cannot all be right, or for that matter, wrong. The main difference between formal religions seems to be the transition process from the physical to the spiritual state, including how and when a soul reaches the afterlife.

With respect, each religion might be reasonably questioned about being self-serving insomuch as each "offers" the "true" (or "only way") to reach Heaven or Paradise.

This book has been written in "good faith" without any religious affiliation. Sources are shown at the end of each chapter.

Whether you're a skeptic or a believer, the book offers a fascinating and engaging exploration of one of life's most enduring mysteries.

Stephen Treloar

Dr. Stephen Treloar
author@lifeafterdeath.au
www.lifeafterdeath.au

Life After Death

— OUR JOURNEY CONTINUES... —

Chapter 1

LIFE AFTER DEATH

Thank you for reading this book. Without wishing to be pedantic, the author believes that "yes," there is a life after death, and reading this book could be a transformative experience for those questioning their beliefs.

The contents of this book are not designed to be confrontational or seek to debate, convince, or convert, and the author has no religious affiliation. The book's objectives are to stimulate contemplation and reflection about the prospect of life after death. The reader will decide for themself or lead to further thoughts on the subject. Consider praying for guidance and revelation for deeper understanding if you are religious.

According to the Pew Research Center, Washington D.C., the world's major religions are Christianity, Islam, Hinduism, Buddhism, Sikhism, and Judaism, each holding the following approximate percentages of the global population as of the time of publication*

Chart 1.1: The World's Greatest Religions

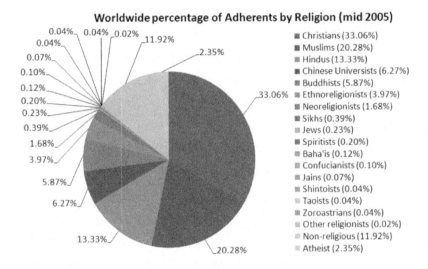

* The information shown in the chart above is based on the estimated percentage of the world's population that affiliates with each of the five major religions based on data from various sources, including the World Religion Database, the Pew Research Center, and the World Factbook by the Central Intelligence Agency (CIA). *Please note that the above percentages are estimates and can vary based on the source and region. Additionally, many people do not affiliate with or practice a religion other than the five major ones, and these numbers should be considered general approximations. The report was published in 2005 and should be read as indicative only.

Heaven and Hell can be traced back to ancient cultures and religions, but it is most commonly associated with the Abrahamic religions, particularly Christianity and Islam. The Bible, the primary text of Christianity, includes numerous references to Heaven and Hell.

Heaven in the Bible is often described as a place of eternal happiness where believers will be reunited with God and live in lasting peace and joy. Conversely, Hell is often described as a place of eternal suffering, where sinners will be punished for their sins.

Some key Bible verses that refer to Heaven include:

- John 14:2-3: *"My Father's house has many rooms; if that were not, would I have told you that I am going there to prepare a place for you? And if I go and prepare a place for you, I will come back and take you to be with me so that you also may be where I am."*

- 1 Corinthians 2:9: *"What no eye has seen, what no ear has heard, and what no human mind has conceived — the things God has prepared for those who love him."*

- Revelation 21:4: *"He will wipe every tear from their eyes. There will be no more death, mourning, crying, or pain, for the old order of things has passed away."*

It's worth noting that the concept of Heaven and Hell has evolved and been interpreted differently over time, both within Christianity and other religions. However, these biblical verses are often cited as the basis for the traditional Christian understanding and justification of these concepts.

The concept of a divine afterlife, where souls go after death, has been present in various forms across many cultures throughout history.

The ancient Egyptians believed in a complex afterlife system where a person's soul would be judged after death and could either go to paradise or be devoured by a monster. The Vikings believed in a heaven called Valhalla, where warriors who died in battle would go. The Greeks had a similar system, where three gods would judge a soul and could go to either the Elysian Fields or Tartarus.

In Christianity, the terms Heaven and Hell were used to describe the ultimate destinations of the souls of the righteous and the wicked, respectively. Earlier beliefs have influenced the concept of Heaven and Hell in Christianity in the afterlife and philosophical and theological ideas that developed over time.

The Christian View – Life After Death – Heaven

In the Christian faith, Heaven is considered a place of perfect joy and peace [1a]. It is a physical place outside Earth [2a], where all good Christians go when they die [1a]. God rules over everyone in Heaven, and everything is done [1a]. As such, those who accept Christ as their savior will be rewarded in Heaven [1a], whereas those who do not will be damned [2a]. The only way to  defend against objections to Heaven's existence is to take those objections seriously, which was strongly advocated for in the nineteenth century in response to the disappearance of Heaven from religious belief [1a]. In the late twentieth century, however, Heaven is slowly fading from faith's horizon

[1a], and those who believe in Heaven but not the afterlife is contradictory in a Christian context [3a].

The Christian View – life after death – Hell

Some key Bible verses that refer to Hell include:

- Matthew 25:41: *"Then he will say to those on his left, 'Depart from me, you who are cursed, into the eternal fire prepared for the devil and his angels.'"*

- Mark 9:47-48: *"And if your eye causes you to stumble, pluck it out. It is better for you to enter the kingdom of God with one eye than to have two eyes and be thrown into hell, where the worms that eat them do not die, and the fire is not quenched."*

- Revelation 20:15: *"Anyone whose name was not found written in the book of life was thrown into the lake of fire."*

According to the Christian faith, Hell is an eternal place of punishment for sinners [4]. It is not a physical place of torture but rather a spiritual one where the souls of the wicked are separated from God's presence and thus subject to torment and anguish. The Bible describes Hell as an "outer darkness" and a "lake of fire" where there will be "weeping and gnashing of teeth" (Matthew 8:12). It is a place of no hope, no mercy, and no escape. Christians believe that Hell is a real place and those who have not accepted Jesus Christ as their Savior will spend eternity in this place of torment and despair. It is where God's wrath and justice are satisfied, and those who have rejected God's love and mercy will experience His judgment. Hell is not a place for God to punish people out of spite, but rather a place of punishment for those who have committed sins against Him and rejected His grace. According to biblical scholars, however, the notion of being Heaven and

16

Hell, as described in the Bible, may have been falsely represented or even perhaps invented and explains *"... many of our ideas about heaven and hell emerged long after Jesus's time, through the struggle to explain the injustices of the world."* [14] (Bart D. Ehrman, 2020). The subject of Heaven and Hell are considered in Chapter 3 of this book.

The Catholic View – life after Death - Purgatory

The concept of purgatory has been debated within the Christian faith for centuries. In the Catholic tradition, purgatory is viewed as a place of spiritual purification, where those who have died in a state of grace may be cleansed of their sins before entering Heaven. This cleansing process is believed to occur in the afterlife and is not viewed as a physical place. Catholic theologians believe that purgatory is a place of temporal punishment, as opposed to the eternal punishment faced by those who die in mortal sin. While many Protestant denominations do not formally recognize the concept of purgatory, some acknowledge the idea of an intermediate state between death and Heaven. In this view, purgatory is a place of spiritual growth and transformation, where those who have died in a state of grace may be prepared for the fullness of life in Heaven. In either case, purgatory is not seen as a place of punishment but rather as an opportunity for spiritual transformation. The Christian view of purgatory is that it is a place of spiritual growth and transformation where those who have died in a state of grace may be prepared for eternal life in Heaven. Of all the teachings of Catholicism, Purgatory is the one most often attacked by Catholics. There are at least three reasons why that is so: many Catholics do not understand the need for Purgatory; they do not understand the scriptural basis for Purgatory, and they have been unintentionally misled by priests and catechism teachers whom themselves do not know what the Catholic Church has taught and continues to teach about Purgatory. Paragraphs 1030-1032 of the Catechism of the Catholic Church. There, in a few short lines, the doctrine of Purgatory is spelled out:

All who die in God's grace and friendship, but are still imperfectly purified, are indeed assured of their eternal salvation. Still, after death, they undergo purification to achieve the holiness necessary to enter the joy of Heaven. (Paragraphs 1030-1032 of the Catechism of the Catholic Church).

The Church gives the name Purgatory to this final purification of the elect, which is entirely different from the punishment of the 'damned.' The Church formulated her doctrine of faith in Purgatory, especially at the Councils of Florence and Trent. One of the lines from the preceding quotation from the Catechism of the Catholic Church—*"to achieve the holiness necessary to enter the joy of Heaven"*—points us in the right direction, but the Catechism offers even more. In the section on indulgences, there are two paragraphs (1472-1473) on *"The punishments of sin":* Catholics believe Purgatory is not a third "final destination," like Heaven and Hell, but merely a place of purification, where those who are *"imperfectly purified . . . undergo purification, to achieve the holiness necessary to enter the joy of Heaven."* (ThoughtCo. "Does the Catholic Church Still Believe in Purgatory?" Learn Religions, Feb. 8, 2021, learnreligions.com/ does-the-catholic-church-still-believe-in-purgatory-4096467) by Thought Co. It was updated on June 25, 2019).

The Islamic View – life after death

In Muslim tradition, a paradise is a place of eternal bliss and joy where physical, mental, and spiritual well-being is enjoyed [5]. It is also a place of peace and harmony [5]. Islamic teachings state that upon death, one's faith is evaluated in a separate dimension of existence that begins at the grave [7]. This is seen as a judgment and a dreamless sleep and can also be seen as a form of  punishment [7]. Interestingly, children of all ages have been found to draw concrete depictions of Heaven, with boys' drawings representing power and girls' depicting love and compassion [6]. As children age, their drawings of Heaven become more abstract and complex [6], indicative of their growing understanding of paradise.

Muslims hold a unique view of judgment, believing that God will judge people based on their intentions, deeds, and faith [9]. This belief is further rooted in Islamic beliefs about the fate of the deceased's body after death. For example, organs are believed to take on an independent role as "witnesses" to an individual's life on Judgement Day [8]. This concept, in part, leads to a fatalistic approach to illness and a fear that the donor would have no control over the probity of the recipient of an organ [8]. Additionally, a belief in the sacredness of the body is derived from the Islamic concept of bodily resurrection [8]. Therefore, the Muslim view of judgment is multifaceted and deeply rooted in Islamic beliefs about the afterlife. Muslims believe that resurrection after death is fundamental to the

Islamic faith [10]. According to Islamic eschatological concepts, the dead will rise after bodily death and be judged based on their deeds before entering paradise or Hell [10]. Although Islamic jurisprudential laws vary from country to country and from one era to another [10], they all share a common belief in the resurrection. However, there are also differences in the interpretation of resurrection among the various sects of Islam [10]. This is because resurrection is considered a part of the unseen side of faith [10] and thus is subject to different interpretations. For example, some believe that time has no meaning after death, while others believe that a person's destiny in Paradise or Hell is determined in the blink of an eye [10]. In any case, resurrection is a core belief in Islam, and Muslims need to understand this concept's various views and interpretations.

The Buddhist View - life after death

Buddhism teaches that the cycle of birth, death, and rebirth (Samsara) continues until one reaches enlightenment and liberation from this cycle. After death, the consciousness is believed to be reborn in another body, either human or non-human. The quality of the next life is determined by the  actions (Karma) in the previous life. The Buddhist view on life after death is based on the teachings of the Four Noble Truths, the Noble Eightfold Path, and the doctrine of rebirth (Samsara). The Four Noble Truths and the Noble Eightfold Path are considered to be the core teachings of Buddhism and are closely related to the idea of life after death. According to the Four Noble Truths, suffering is an inherent part of life; however, it can be overcome by observing the Noble Eightfold Path. According to Buddhist

20

teachings, rebirth or Samsara is an important aspect of life after death. Samsara is a cycle of death and resurrection, in which each life lived is determined by the Karma earned in past lives. The Noble Eightfold Path, which consists of the right understanding, right thought, right speech, right action, right livelihood, right effort, right mindfulness, and right concentration, is a path to understanding the cause of suffering and ultimately ending that suffering through the cessation of Karma [1]. This path is meant to guide and guide how to live an ethical and moral life to break the cycle of rebirth and achieve a state of Nirvana [2]. [3] This view is widely documented in Buddhist scriptures, such as the Pali Canon, the Mahayana Sutras, and the Tibetan Book of the Dead.

The Hinduism View – Life after Death

In Hinduism, the belief in life after death varies among sects, but the cycle of reincarnation, or Samsara, is a central belief. It is believed that after death, the soul is reborn in a new body, and the nature and circumstances of this rebirth are determined by the Karma, or actions, of the previous life. Many Hindus aim to break the cycle of  reincarnation and achieve Moksha, or liberation from birth and death.

The information provided on Hinduism's beliefs about life after death is based on a general understanding of Hinduism and its central tenets as they have been recorded in sacred Hindu texts such as the Vedas, the Bhagavad Gita, and the Puranas, as well as interpreted and taught by scholars and leaders within the religion. It is worth noting that the beliefs and practices within Hinduism can vary among different sects and regions and that this information should be considered a general overview rather than a comprehensive representation of all Hindu beliefs.

The Sikhism View – life after death

Sikhism teaches that the soul is an immortal spark of the divine. At death, the soul departs the physical body and is judged based on its actions in life. The soul then temporarily goes to Heaven or Hell before reincarnation into another body. This cycle of birth, death, and rebirth continues until the soul merges back with the ultimate reality (Waheguru). The goal in Sikhism is to live a virtuous life, follow the teachings of the Guru, and attain union with Waheguru, thus breaking the cycle of reincarnation and reaching a state of liberation (Mukti).

This information is based on the fundamental beliefs and teachings of Sikhism as outlined in the Sikh scriptures, the Guru Granth Sahib, and is widely accepted among the Sikh community. It reflects a general understanding of the religion and may vary in interpretation among individuals and different sects within Sikhism.

The Judaism View – life after death

The Jewish view of the afterlife is complex and multifaceted. It is one of the most debated topics amongst Jews, with different sects having different interpretations and beliefs. The Jewish view of the afterlife focuses less on a physical or spiritual afterlife than other religions. Instead, Jewish tradition emphasizes the importance of positively impacting this life rather than worrying about what comes after. Jewish wisdom does not provide a definitive answer as to what happens when we die and if we will see our loved ones. [1b] In traditional Judaism, Heaven is not a place off-limits to anyone; instead, it is open to all who live righteous and moral lives [2b]. It is also possible to believe that the souls of the righteous dead go to a place similar to the Christian idea of Heaven or that they are reincarnated in another life [3b]. Ultimately, Jewish wisdom encourages us to focus on living our lives in a way that will bring us closer to God rather than worrying about the afterlife. In this sense, the afterlife is seen as a reward for living a good life and doing honorable deeds in this world.

The Talmud, a collection of Jewish texts, states that after death, the soul goes to Sheol, a place of rest and peace. This is often seen as a spiritual afterlife, where the soul is judged based on the deeds performed in life. The Jewish view of the afterlife is complex and varied, with different sects having different beliefs and interpretations. For some Jews, the afterlife is seen as a place of spiritual growth where the soul can continue to learn and grow. For others, the afterlife is seen as a time to be reunited with loved ones who have passed away.

Further Reading :

- *1b.https://reformjudaism.org*
- *2b. https://momentmag.com*
- *3b. https://www.jewfaq.org*

The Church of Jesus Christ of Latter-day Saints. View on life after death.

Importance of their name. The official name is the Church of Jesus Christ of Latter-Day – Saints. A name derived from a belief in a revelation from God to Joseph Smith in 1838. The term Mormons (including 'Mormonism') is not

offensive to followers but mistakenly used in its application as the name of their Church (and its followers). Confusion arose from one of the Church's texts, the Book of Mormon. (source: www.churchofjesuschrist.org)

The 'Heavenly Father' concept is integral to many religions, especially Abrahamic traditions [3]. This is a notion of a divine parent, a loving, caring, and just God, who watches over and protects His children on Earth [1]. The Heavenly Father is the God of Christianity, Islam, Judaism, and other religions [3]. In the Latter-day Saint tradition, the Heavenly Father is the spirit of the Father, who is God [2]. It is believed that God was once a man on another planet before being exalted to Godhood [2]. According to Latter-day Saint scripture and modern prophecy, there is a Heavenly Mother and a Heavenly Father [3]. This divine partnership is referred to as the Heavenly Father [2]. Latter-day Saints believe that Heavenly Father is the literal Father of our spirits, and God's use of the name "Father" teaches us the importance of family and love [1]. God has commanded us to pray to Him, whom we know as our Heavenly Father, and He uses the name "Father" when referring to Himself [1]. Joseph Smith taught that we are spirit offspring of God, literally [1] and that the Father, Son and Holy Spirit constitute the "supreme power over all things" [2]. Thus, the Heavenly Father is the God of the Son and the Holy Spirit, the God of Christianity, the God of the Bible, the God of the Holy Spirit, the God of the Son, the God of the New Testament, the God of all religions, and the God of the Abrahamic religions [2][3].

The resurrection of Jesus Christ is a central tenet of the Latter-day Saint faith. This belief holds that all humanity will be eternally resurrected and reunited with their spirits [4]. This is based on the words of the Apostle Paul, who spoke of three Heavens or degrees of post-resurrection glory [4]. Mormons believe that the first resurrection occurred at the moment of Christ's resurrection [4] when the righteous of past ages were resurrected. The second resurrection will appear at the Second Coming of Jesus Christ, and the last resurrection is reserved for the wicked [4]. Mormons believe that the resurrected Christ is the most glorious of all resurrected beings [4] and that all human beings are guaranteed resurrection after death [7]. However, how those resurrected beings experience resurrection is determined by the actions and desires of the individual [6]. The Telestial Kingdom is for those with endless punishment, the Terrestrial Kingdom is for those who live after death, and the Celestial Kingdom is for those with eternal families [5]. Ultimately, Mormons believe all will be reunited with their body and spirit after the final judgment [5].

The concept of 'degrees of glory' is essential to Mormon cosmology. According to this belief system, there are three kingdoms of glory: the celestial, terrestrial, and telestial kingdoms [10]. Within the Heavenly realm are three degrees,  and those who inherit the highest degree will dwell in the presence of God the Father and His Son, Jesus Christ [10]. To be exalted to the highest degree and remain in eternity with family relationships, one must enter into the new and everlasting covenant of marriage [10]. The glory we attain in the afterlife is determined by the depth of our conversion and obedience to the Lord's commandments and our commitment to the testimony of Jesus [10].

The terrestrial kingdom is the second degree, symbolically represented by the moon [9][8]. People who will inhabit the terrestrial realm include those who were honorable but blinded by the craftiness of men and members of the Church who were not valiant in the testimony of Jesus [10]. The lowest degree of glory is the telestial kingdom, symbolically represented by stars [9]. Each person's glory in the telestial kingdom will vary depending on their works while on the earth, and there are different degrees of glory within this kingdom [9]. Ultimately, the prize we receive in the afterlife is determined by our righteousness and commitment to the gospel of Jesus Christ [8].

Further Reading :

1. https://mormonbeliefs.org/mormon_beliefs/who-is-jesus-christ/mormons-believe-Heavenly-father/
2. https://en.wikipedia.org/wiki/God_in_Mormonism
3. https://www.fairlatterdaysaints.org/answers/Mormonism_and_the_nature_of_God
4. https://mormonbeliefs.org/mormon_beliefs/mormon-doctrine-salvation/do-mormons-believe-in-the-resurrection/
5. https://www.cru.org/us/en/train-and-grow/spiritual-growth/core-christian-beliefs/what-happens-when-you-die.html
6. https://www.churchofjesuschrist.org/comeuntochrist/africacentral/beliefs/life-after-death
7. https://www.bbc.co.uk/religion/religions/mormon/beliefs/salvation_1.shtml
8. https://www.mormonwiki.com/Celestial,_Terrestrial,_and_Telestial_Kingdoms

The Seven-Day Adventist's View - life after death

Seven-Day Adventists believe in a literal interpretation of the Bible, affecting their views on life after death. They believe in a physical resurrection of the dead on the day of judgment, that the saved will experience eternal life in the Kingdom of Heaven, and that the wicked will experience eternal death

in the Lake of Fire. They also believe that the dead are unconscious until the resurrection and that the soul and spirit go to various locations after death. Specifically, the soul goes to the bosom of Abraham, while the heart goes to God. Finally, they believe that the souls of the righteous will be reunited with their bodies at the resurrection. All these beliefs stem from their literal interpretation of the Bible and are fundamental to their faith.

The Pentecostalists' View – life after death

Pentecostalists believe in the continuation of life after death and the resurrection of the dead. They hold that when a person dies, their spirit goes either to be with the Lord in Heaven or to a state of separation from God, awaiting the final judgment. They believe in the bodily resurrection of the dead at the second coming of Jesus Christ and that the dead will be raised either to eternal life in Heaven or eternal damnation in Hell. This belief is based on their interpretation of biblical passages such as John 5:28-29, 1 Corinthians 15:51-52, and Revelation 20:11-15.

Further Reading :

"What Do Pentecostals Believe ?" Assemblies of God USA (Official Website).

"The Fundamentals of Pentecostal Theology" by Thomas E. Trask and Wayde I. Miles (book on Pentecostal theology).

The Scientology View – life after death

In Scientology, it is believed that the individual is a spiritual being ("Thetan") reincarnated multiple times and gone through many lives. Scientology aims to achieve spiritual enlightenment and become clear, which frees the Thetan from the cycle of birth and death and allows them to exist in eternal spiritual existence. The beliefs about life after death in Scientology are based on the teachings of its founder, L. Ron Hubbard, documented in various Scientology texts, including "Dianetics: The Modern Science of Mental Health" and "The Scientology Handbook." These beliefs are not widely accepted or recognized outside of the Scientology community.

The Jehovah's Witnesses' View – life after Death.

Jehovah's Witnesses believe that after death, the soul ceases to exist, and only the body remains unconscious until the time of the resurrection. They think that at this time, a person will either be resurrected and allowed eternal life on paradise earth or, if wicked and die without repentance, they will be destroyed and cease to exist. This belief is based on their interpretation of biblical passages such as Ecclesiastes 9:5, John 5:28-29, and Revelation 21:1-5. Jehovah's Witnesses believe that only a limited number of people, specifically 144,000, will go to heaven to rule with Jesus Christ in his kingdom (Revelation 7:4; 14:1-4). This belief is based on their interpretation of several biblical passages, including Revelation 14:1-3, which describes a group of 144,000 people "redeemed from the earth" and "purchased from among mankind as first fruits to God and the Lamb."

Those chosen to go to heaven are a special group of faithful Christians who have been called by God and have demonstrated their loyalty by obeying his commands and spreading the gospel message. They believe these individuals will be given immortal, heavenly bodies, and reign with Christ over the earth, helping restore it to a paradise state.

For most Jehovah's Witnesses, who are not part of the 144,000, the hope is to live forever on a restored paradise earth (Psalm 37:11, 29). They believe that God will resurrect the righteous and the unrighteous after

Armageddon. Those deemed worthy will be able to live forever in perfect health and happiness on a paradise earth.

Further Reading:

- *"What Do Jehovah's Witnesses Believe About the Afterlife?" JW.org (Official Website of Jehovah's Witnesses).*

- *"Revelation--Its Grand Climax At Hand!" 1988, pages 178-179 (book published by the Watch Tower Bible and Tract Society of Pennsylvania).*

- *"What Does the Bible Teach?" - published by Jehovah's Witnesses, this book provides an overview of their beliefs, including their understanding of the 144,000 and the hope of living on a paradise earth.*

- *"Insight on the Scriptures" - another publication by Jehovah's Witnesses that provides detailed explanations of various biblical passages, including those related to the 144,000.*

- *jw.org - Jehovah's Witnesses official website provides a wealth of information about their beliefs and practices.*

The Spiritualist View – life after death

Spiritualists believe in the continuation of life after death and communication between the living and the dead. They hold that death is not the end of individual consciousness and that the spirits of the deceased can communicate with the living through mediumship. This belief is based on the idea that the soul is immortal and that there is a spirit world where deceased individuals continue to exist. Spiritualists hold that this spirit world is a place of growth and development where spirits can evolve and progress. Spiritualism is a diverse set of beliefs and practices that revolve around the idea that there is a spiritual realm beyond the physical world and that this realm can be accessed through spiritual practices or communication with spirits. Some spiritualists believe in a monotheistic God, while others believe in multiple gods or a more pantheistic view of the divine.

One core belief of spiritualism is that the soul survives physical death and that communication with the deceased is possible. Spiritualists may use mediumship, divination, or trance states to connect with spirits and receive their messages or guidance.

Many spiritualists also emphasize personal growth and development, seeking to improve themselves and the world through spiritual practices, meditation, and service to others. Some may also believe in the power of positive thinking or the law of attraction, which holds that one's thoughts and beliefs can shape one's reality.

Overall, spiritualism is a diverse and multifaceted belief system that emphasizes connecting with the spiritual realm and striving for personal growth and development.

Further reading:

- *"What Is Spiritualism?" National Spiritualist Association of Churches (NSAC).*
- *"The Principles of Spiritualism" National Spiritualist Association of Churches.*

- *"The Spiritualist Movement: Speaking with the Dead in America and Around the World" by Christopher M. Moreman.*
- *"Spiritualism: A Very Short Introduction" by J. Gordon Melton.*
- *"The Encyclopedia of Ghosts and Spirits" by Rosemary Ellen Guiley.*
- *"The Spirits' Book" by Allan Kardec.*
- *"Modern Spiritualism: A History and a Criticism" by Frank Podmor*

From a Scientific Method view – life after death

The concept of life after death is a topic that has been debated and discussed throughout human history and across diverse cultures and religions. It is often referred to as an afterlife or the immortal soul. In many religious beliefs, life after death is considered a spiritual existence beyond physical reality, where the soul continues to exist and may be subject to judgment and reward or punishment. In other beliefs, death is considered the end of consciousness, and there is no afterlife.

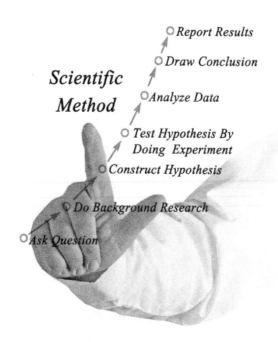

The scientific method's perspective on life after death is that it is currently impossible to prove or disprove its existence and that there is no evidence. The question of what happens after death remains one of the great mysteries of human existence and is a matter of personal belief and faith. This information reflects a widely held view among the scientific community, which is based on the current state of scientific understanding and the lack of empirical evidence for the existence of an afterlife or the soul beyond physical death. This perspective is supported by the scientific method, which relies on empirical evidence and testable explanations. It has yet to find any evidence that supports the existence of an afterlife or a soul within these restraints of scientific protocol. It is a general understanding established through decades of research and discussion in philosophy, religion, and science. However, scientists shocked the world by proving that life after death may exist [1a] [2a]. More recently, near-death experiences have been more intensively studied, and there is some evidence that people may experience consciousness when doctors don't expect them to [3a]. While more research is certainly needed, this is an exciting study area gaining momentum.

Sources :

- 1a. *https://www.irishmirror.ie*
- 2a. *https://www.nvas.org*
- 3a. *https://www.livescience.com*

Summary of Christian View on life after death

The Christian concept of an afterlife is based on the teachings of Jesus Christ. He taught that believers would go to eternal bliss after death. Jesus also taught that whatever a person did in this life would determine their destiny in the next. For this reason, some have interpreted his teachings to mean that people can bring themselves to Heaven or Hell through their behavior. Other interpretations hold that there is no Hell or salvation outside of Christ's sacrifice for sins. Either way, the belief that humans have power over their fate in an afterlife has led to conflict between believers and non-believers.

Many early Christians believed that Jesus' death on the cross paid for all human sins. This belief led to the concept of 'atonement,' which became part of official Christian doctrine in the 4th century AD. However, many modern Christians reject this doctrine, stating that Jesus' death did not fully atone for human sin. When a person accepts Christ as his savior, the process of being forgiven by God is complete for the last time. But this does not mean that human beings can ever truly turn themselves away from God; they must still accept His forgiveness or be forever separated from Him.

Since early Christianity was persecuted, many early Christians believed that the end of time was near. They expected a great resurrection to occur at the end of time, after which all dead people would be resurrected into the Heavenly realms. Joseph Smith later referred to this expectation as 'conditional immortality' since some early Christians believed that resurrection into Heaven depended on a person's behavior in this life. The idea was that if a person lived righteously, he would enter eternal bliss; if he lived wrongous, he could end up in Hell instead. It was later revealed that 'conditional immortality' is not what God intended for human beings. It is now understood that our spiritual status is linked to our standing with God from birth- through- death and beyond.

The concept of an afterlife is not always harmonious among Christians because it depends largely on what religious leaders tell their followers about paradise and Hell. Early Christianity was generally hostile to Roman Imperialism and pagan beliefs like Mithraism, which were popular among soldiers and citizens alike during the Roman Empire's decline. Many early Christians interpreted Roman paganism as leading them astray into a false resurrection system similar to what they had rejected before. For this reason, many early Christians expected a resurrection after the crucifixion of Christ to take place alongside the resurrection of Jesus himself. However, when neither group reappeared, some began to doubt Christ's Resurrection and his future role as judge of humanity's fate. Eventually, though, most came around to accepting these things as 'partivity' (*Ed: meaning the quality of being able to be divided into equal parts)* of Christ's sacrifice on the cross. As such, accepting Christ - through faith - now leads to salvation no matter how one's behavior may have previously affected one's earthly fate.

Some might argue that accepting another being as one's savior negates one's power over one's fate in the afterlife. This is not necessarily so; most

Christians view their savior as just another aspect of their relationship with God- even though they view their savior as having come from them rather than God himself. In other words, they view their savior as being created by them rather than being part of the Creator Himself. Whether one considers a salvable person as having summoned or received his savior himself lacks any real importance since both viewpoints acknowledge that salvation is not something granted by any mortal entity but rather received by grace through faith in Christ's atonement on the cross.

The teachings of Jesus concerning an afterlife form the basis for most Christian beliefs regarding this subject matter. Though Heaven and Hell are popular concepts, Latter-day Saints believe in something different based on their interpretation of biblical teachings concerning death and resurrection.

Summary of this Chapter

Life after death is a major theme in many religions and philosophies. It is a central tenet of many belief systems, but its veracity has been debated. Many people believe in life after death but do not know what happens when we die. They are curious and often look for ways to do so.

One way to experience life after death is through a near-death experience (NDE). People who underwent an NDE said they had visited a place they could not describe. They saw deceased family members, friends, and other entities they knew were dead. They also saw scenes from their lives when they were healthy, as well as those when they were near death. Some NDErs even met deceased persons who had not yet crossed over but were now ready to do so. This experience has inspired many to believe in life after death.

Other people have had personal visions or experiences showing that death is only a transition to another form or state of life. For example, some believe mediums can contact the spirits of the dead and ask them questions. There is no scientific proof that contact with or by the afterlife is possible, although an increasing number of people are not so sure to dismiss what is said to them based on predictions that have materialized. Mediums generally receive answers usually in line with Christian teachings, although the Bible advises not to communicate with 'familiar' spirits, with the word familiar once meaning 'evil' spirits. Also, mediums generally hear confirmation from the spirit world that Jesus Christ was born to save us from our sins and were crucified for those same sins. This experience leads many to believe in life after death because it confirms their faith in God and Jesus Christ.

Despite these personal experiences and visions, some who have had NDE do not believe in life after death for various reasons. For some people, believing in life after death contradicts their religious beliefs and values. This can be upsetting since many people base their moral codes on what they learned as children in church or at home. Many also fear that believing in life after death would mean accepting evil spirits or demonic possession.

Other reasons people do not believe in life after death include the belief that scientific advancements show that death is the end of all physical matter; it goes back into the ground or melts into oblivion or non-existence; some believe there is no other realm beyond this physical one.

Some people do not believe in life after death for various reasons, and the concept can be overwhelming. However, many statistically significant persons who have experienced NDE strongly believe they have shared a glimpse of the afterlife and 'return' with profound changes to their view of life, relationships, and an awareness of God.

The Author's View – life after death

Despite the enormity of the question and your reflection on whether there is 'life after death,' it does not matter - the truth of the Mystery of Life will be revealed to each of us at our life-end. The author expresses the view that there is 'life after death' awaiting us all. This is also in alignment with the teachings of the afterlife in most major religions - with one major difference! Most, if not all, major religions pronounce their instructions as the 'only' way to find Heaven/Paradise/Nirvana in the afterlife; by definition, this means that if one does not follow the teaching of a particular brand of religion – they will not enter Heaven/Paradise/Nirvana. The author respects all viewpoints but believes otherwise. There are no 'winners' or 'losers' to enter the afterlife based on following the 'right' brand of faith or religion. All will be received equally, regardless of their religious following, including those without religion or knowledge of God. Purity of heart, quality of character, and compassion for others - will be a greater determinant than the parochial religious belief of who you 'arrived through.'

The acquired earthly riches will not determine the value of your life contribution and secure your place in Heaven, nor will titles, spheres of influence, or power. It is not a question of what you achieved in life but how you used whatever you had for the benefit of others. This might be rounded down to the degree of love you shared in your life. It is said God is Love; then suggestively, this might be the ultimate measure of contribution in life.

This author's view is that you will see in Heaven the entity you expect to see, whether known as God, the Light, Allah, Father, Lord, Yahwweh, the Almighty, the Creator, Holy Spirit, King of Kings, Infinite Spirit, Jehovah, or other such names. Christians arriving in the afterlife will seek to 'see' Jesus, and those of other religions will seek to recognize their deity.

A positive aspect of being part of a formalized religion is the opportunity to meet and share a communion of faith in "God" and recognize a much higher essence in their lives. Not to place egocentrically 'themselves' as the focal point of the universe but driven by higher-order values towards humankind.

There is much mystery about what happens to a soul or spirit on arrival to the afterlife. Spiritualists speak of a series of planes where a spirit naturally gravitates to others of their liking. If, for example, there are nine planes, then the higher the level of the plane, the nearer to God shall be. The lower the plane are those of lower inclinations, and the lowest is of evil. The Jewish angelic hierarchy is established in the Hebrew Bible, Talmud, Rabbinic literature, whose texts report on the 'Nine Hierarchy of Angels". Throughout the Holy Bible, there are angels ("spirits') who confer with those in the physical world. The word itself, angel, derives from the Greek "angelos," a translation of a Hebrew word meaning "messenger." Hence when spirits (Angels) make their presence known to the living, especially to loved ones, they are 'messengers' from the afterlife.

More of this question is considered in Chapter 9.

Finally, the obverse to a belief in life after death is that there is nothing after death but human flesh deteriorating, and the person is no more; their soul or spirit is also no more (or never existed in the first place). Some religions believe in reincarnation, where the soul goes on into another person (newborn baby) or another living organism (see Chapter Reincarnation).

The author believes that our time on earth has a purpose, and when we die, there is a separation of our physical body and soul (or spirit). The significant findings of thousands upon thousands of independently investigated cases of persons pronounced dead on the operating table, only to be revived with vivid memories of NDE, cannot be ignored, especially substantial reports of similarity of experience. This has provided researchers with a glimpse of 'life after death.' Many who experienced an NDE are left with life-changing revelations. There have been over fifty years of scientific investigations into NDE, with the University of Virginia leading. The work by Professor Bruce Greyson, M.D., and his team, have been some of the leaders in this field of research. Some of their remarkable findings are shared in a later chapter of this book, and the author thanks Professor Greyson for his kind permission to share some of his amazing investigative research team findings in this book.

The contentious question of there being a Heaven or Hell and whether they exist is also considered in a later chapter of this book, and the author thanks and acknowledges the kind permission of Professor Bart D. Ehrman, a religious scholar, for allowing the inclusion in this tome of research findings reported in his revealing book: "Heaven and Hell – A History of the Afterlife." [14]

The author believes there is no absolute Heaven and Hell (only a position of closeness to God (or the Light) or distance/separation from the Light. The natural principle of 'like attracting like' suggests a spirit might go to a level where they share similarities of like with others. The Bible speaks of Jesus in John 14, "In my Father's house are many mansions: if it were not so, I would have told you. I am going to prepare a place for you. And if I go and prepare a place for you, I will come again, and receive you unto myself; that where I am, there ye may also be" (John 14:1-3). The original meaning of "mansions" retranslates now to mean "rooms" in contemporary vernacular, may also be suggesting levels, or planes within Heaven, with the upper planes being with God in Heaven, spiraling downwards to echoes the popular perception of Hell.

The next Chapter considers the Meaning of Life.

Sources :

1. *https://link.springer.com/chapter/10.1057/9780230375970_4*

2. *https://www.jstor.org/stable/2657404*

3. *https://www.jstor.org/stable/3509882*

4. *https://link.springer.com/chapter/10.1057/9780230375970_4*

5. *https://www.jstor.org/stable/2657404*

6. *https://www.jstor.org/stable/3509882*

7. *https://www.sciencedirect.com/science/article/pii/S0092656604001096*

8. *https://www.jstor.org/stable/2083285*

9. *https://link.springer.com/article/10.1007/s11089-021-00958-1*

10. *https://www.taylorfrancis.com/chapters/edit/10.4324/9781315545349-28/afterlife-deathan-islamic-perspective-david-oualaalou*

11. *https://www.sciencedirect.com/science/article/pii/S1600613522036887*

12. *https://link.springer.com/chapter/10.1007/978-3-319-05873-3_2*

13. *https://www.mdpi.com/183024*

14. *https://www.taylorfrancis.com/books/mono/10.4324/9781315238258/mormon-culture-salvation-douglas-davies*

15. *https://link.springer.com/chapter/10.1057/978-1-137-48609-7_22*

16. *https://www.jstor.org/stable/3511418*

17. *Ehrman, Bart, D. (2020). Heaven and Hell, A History of the Afterlife, Oneworld, London.*

Life After Death

—OUR JOURNEY CONTINUES...—

Chapter 2

THE MEANING OF LIFE

The meaning of life is a philosophical question debated throughout human history by scholars, theologians, and thinkers from various cultural and ideological backgrounds. There is no single, universally accepted answer, as the meaning of life is subjective and can vary greatly depending on an individual's beliefs, values, and experiences.

It is normal to think about "Why are we here ?" "What is my life's purpose ?" and "Is that all there is ?" Alternatively, some may not think about the question and respond with the words, "It is what it is." Some firmly believe that life has no purpose and that we are all here as a product of nature.

What is the source of our existence ?

For centuries, humans have sought to explain the source of our existence. While religious apologists have long argued that God is the source of moral obligations, this "raw" explanation has been challenged in recent years [4]. The argument that moral laws are God's commands is undermined by the fact that people aware of moral obligations are aware of God's commands without realizing that they are God's commands, a grave problem for religious apologists [4]. The fact that moral laws can be explained through the authority of legislatures (or absolute monarchs in some countries) who have the power to pass such laws is the best argument against the religious apologist's claim [4]. Despite this, many still cling to the belief that God is the best candidate to fulfill the role of explaining the existence of moral laws [4]. Some suggest that the universe had a beginning, is expanding, and will eventually end [4]. This means that our origins likely include a functional equivalent of a terminus or a parcel [6] and that our existence is ultimately a result of natural forces. We should celebrate this truth, as it provides us with a life-enhancing understanding of our existence [6], enabling us to modify our current life [5]. With insight into our biological heritage, we can appreciate the minimal requirements for life, such as physical activity, food, and reproduction, that have been conditions of human life for millions of years, and we can recognize the importance of the body at rest as well as during exercise [5].

What does it mean to have a life ?

To have a life is an expression used immemorial and holds deep meaning. Fundamentally, having a life is about having purpose and feeling fulfilled [7]. The presence of meaning in life is thought to have direct and indirect effects on an individual's overall well-being [7]. Direct effects are associated with greater psychological distress, whereas indirect effects are related to better psychological health [7]. Meaning in life is also associated with the greater search for meaning, which indicates lower psychological distress and more positive direct effects of having a life on the individual [7]. At its core, having a life is about having a sense of meaning [7]. This sense of purpose refers to the presence of, and significance felt regarding, the nature of one's being and existence. It is also about experiencing positive and negative aspects, points, characteristics, values, characteristics, consequences, outcomes, moments, consequences, and effects and embarking on a unique, ongoing journey towards a desired end state [7].

Furthermore, life is about having positive and negative elements, good and bad moments, positive and negative experiences, and the sum of all the experiences and memories that make up a person's existence [7]. This sense of purpose, the feeling that one's life is goal-oriented

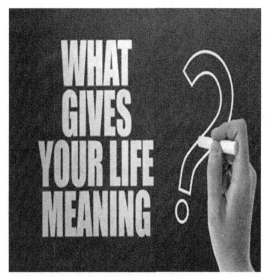

and driven, tends to be protective of psychological health. However, less is known about its relationship with social health, particularly loneliness [7]. Whether or how well one's purpose matches one's life's goals determines whether one will develop incident loneliness over time [7]. To better understand life's meaning, philosophical, theoretical, and empirical psychology each has its components of work. A life design is a positive life approach incorporating these components [7]. A longitudinal study investigating whether recognition of meaning in life (MIL) at baseline confers resiliency to the onset and exacerbation of suicide ideation over a 6- to 22-month period of follow-up has found that gratitude and grit synergistically confer resiliency to suicide by increasing meaning in life [7]. Nevertheless, a meaningful life may be hard to modify directly as we seek to live a good and right life, striving for a significant, fulfilling life with a purpose. [7]

Extraversion and neuroticism are important aspects of life. Research findings indicate that situational meaningfulness is a negative predictor of state loneliness and that the perceived meaning of activity is negatively associated with loneliness. That life engagement is negatively associated with trait loneliness [7]. Additionally, research findings indicate that loneliness is proportional to the meaninglessness of activity [7]. Late-life suicide ideation is a theoretical model of the onset and exacerbation of late-life suicide ideation that considers risk, resiliency, and precipitating factors [7]. All in all, life is about having a sense of purpose and fulfillment.

What is the purpose of life on earth according to God ?

According to most of the world's religious teachings, God's plan, and the purpose of life on Earth are to serve Him. God is the Creator and Master of the universe, having arranged everything to fulfill His will [8]. Most religions contend that all life on earth, including humans, was created by Him [8]. The ultimate purpose of our lives is to glorify and serve God, to love Him, and to live in a way that pleases Him. This is the ultimate truth that God has revealed to us. We are instructed to seek to understand God's will and follow it in our lives. We must strive to live in harmony with God and His creation. We must also strive to honor and obey God's laws so that we may live a life that is pleasing to Him. By doing this, we can fulfill the purpose of life on earth according to God.

46

Big Bang Theory of Creation

Opposed to the creationist idea of how the world began from the Holy Bible falls into what has been termed the 'Big Bang' theory, which is the prevailing cosmological model for the creation of the observable universe. Sources the reader might like to follow up on are summarized below:

1. NASA: The official website of the National Aeronautics and Space Administration (NASA) provides a wealth of information on the Big Bang theory. It presents a scientific explanation of the universe's origins, the cosmic microwave background radiation, and its expansion. Here is the link: https://www.nasa.gov/audience/forstudents/k-4/stories/nasa-knows/what-is-the-big-bang-k4.html

2. Stanford Encyclopedia of Philosophy: The Stanford Encyclopedia of Philosophy is a great resource for learning about philosophical concepts related to the Big Bang theory. Here is the link: https://plato.stanford.edu/entries/cosmology/

3. CERN: The European Organization for Nuclear Research (CERN) is a major center for studying particle physics. Their website provides information on the early universe and the role of particle physics in understanding the Big Bang. Here is the link: https://home.cern/science/physics/early-universe

4. Scientific American: Scientific American is a popular science magazine covering many topics, including the Big Bang theory. They provide articles written by experts in the field, as well as news and analysis on the latest developments in cosmology. Here is the link: https://www.scientificamerican.com/article/the-big-bang-theory-of-the-universe-a-beginners-guide/

5. "The Big Bang: A Very Short Introduction" by Katherine Blundell: This book provides a concise and accessible introduction to the Big Bang theory. It covers the history of the idea, the evidence supporting it, and the current debates and challenges in the field.

What is God's expectation from humans ?

What does God expect from humanity ? According to the Bible, God expects a lot from us. He expects us to treat each other with respect, to live in harmony with each other and the natural world, and to use our potential to be like Him [9]. The Bible also tells us that God expects us to be honest and compassionate and show mercy and forgiveness to those who have wronged us. God also expects us to love our neighbors as ourselves, to be generous with our time and resources, and to be willing to serve others. Ultimately, God desires that we would love Him and seek to do His will. As our Creator and Father, He wants us to obey His commandments and live lives that reflect His love and grace. Essentially, God expects us to live lives that honor and bring Him glory.

Many religious traditions provide answers to the question of the meaning of life, such as the belief in a divine purpose or afterlife. In contrast, others offer more secular or humanistic explanations focusing on the individual's experience, relationships, and impact on the world.

In philosophy, various schools of thought offer different perspectives on the meaning of life ; one is existentialism, a philosophical movement that emphasizes individual freedom and choice in the search for meaning and purpose in life. Existentialists argue that life has no inherent meaning and that it is up to each person to give their life meaning through their experiences and relationships. It asserts that a sense of absurdity characterizes human existence and that individuals must create meaning through their choices and actions.

Nihilism is another philosophical viewpoint that suggests life lacks inherent meaning, purpose, or value. Nihilists reject traditional beliefs and values and argue that existence is ultimately meaningless.

48

Stoicism is a philosophy that originated in ancient Greece and emphasized the development of self-control, courage, wisdom, and justice. Stoics believe that rational laws govern the universe and that individuals can find meaning and fulfillment by conforming to these laws and living a life of virtue. They also think accepting life's challenges and difficulties with equanimity and grace is essential to finding meaning and purpose in life.

Meaning of life according to new age spirituality

What, indeed, can the meaning of life be to those who claim to believe in the mysterious and infinite nature of the universe ?

Those who believe in spirituality understand that the Universe, like the numeric system, is infinite by nature. God is, thus, unknowable through any sound system of understanding, just as one cannot hope ever to understand the entirety of the numeric system using reason or logic. The conclusive "infinity," which encompasses the whole of the numeric system, and indeed the universe, holds the answer, which is philosophical or spiritual.

When discussing infinity, we must use our faculties of intuition. Indeed, the duality of necessity with both logic and intuition/emotion is significant. The meaning of life or experiences, in general, may only be gleaned by utilizing both faculties in conjunction. The numeric system articulates and expresses infinity. However, forever is from which the numeric system originated and is the entirety of it. We may apply this to our manifested universe. All the manifestations of creation (including you and me) are expressions or articulations of an infinite source or God, which this single principle may encapsulate. Thus, infinity may also be the principle of Unity. It is everything, yet one single thing.

This is completely different from the general belief in popular traditions that God stands separate and above the rest of their creation.

This is an example of how we have, over the years, begun to personify this one thing, injecting it with personalities and various aspects, which is where historically, artificial "gods" emerge to explain every phenomenon. Eventually, interestingly we have unified creation under a single god yet have personified him as an entity rather than the entirety of what has been.

THE MEANING OF LIFE IS TO FIND YOUR GIFT. THE PURPOSE OF LIFE IS TO GIVE IT AWAY.

How does one find the meaning of their own life?

Finding the meaning of life is a complex and personal process that can be influenced by many factors, such as one's beliefs, values, and experiences. Here are some approaches and sources that may help find the meaning of life:

1. Self-reflection: Ask yourself what brings you joy, your passions, and your values. Spend time in solitude and write down your thoughts and feelings. Reflect on your past experiences and consider what lessons you've learned from them.

2. Seek guidance from a spiritual or religious leader: If you're religious, you may want to seek advice from a spiritual or religious leader. They can help you explore the teachings and principles of your faith and how they relate to the meaning of life.

3. Read books and philosophical texts: Many books and philosophical texts explore the meaning of life. Some examples include "Man's

Search for Meaning" by Viktor Frankl, "The Republic" by Plato, and "The Tao Te Ching" by Lao Tzu.

4. Talk to a therapist: A therapist can help you explore your thoughts and feelings and guide you in finding meaning in life. They can also help you develop coping skills for life's challenges.

5. Volunteer and help others: Helping others can give you a sense of purpose and meaning. Volunteer at a local charity or community organization and see how you can make a difference in the lives of others.

Remember, finding the meaning of life is a personal journey, and there's no one-size-fits-all approach. Be patient and take the time to explore what matters most to you.

Author's view on the meaning of life

Finding the meaning of life is often underpinned by a person's religious belief and arguably shapes an expectation of attitude, behavior, and observance. Within this myriad, a person seeks meaning or purpose in life. Whether one believes or does not believe in another person's religion, this author suggests, it doesn't matter as the follower is removing their ego of self to a higher order. When someone places themselves as the center of their life, they will come up short. The meaning and purpose of life will not be found in looking at oneself as the center but in the quality of their character to help others less fortunate and those with greater need than themselves.

To discover an understanding of the meaning of life might be boldly summarized as follows :

Firstly, to remove oneself as the center of the universe and observe the needs of others surrounding you. You might accrue wealth, fame, title, recognition, and power, but none will provide you with the joy, peace, and serenity you seek. The meaning of your life will not be found in self-aggrandizement but in sharing and using your skills to assist the less fortunate. For example, I have legal friends who work for large international law firms; they tell me they most enjoy, albeit only one day (or so) per month, being allowed to perform pro-bono services to the disadvantaged. This includes visiting and advising people experiencing homelessness on matters of a legal nature or assisting with financial or legal counseling as needed. In other words, performing in the profession they were trained in but also are of service to others.

There is so much need in society within and beyond your national borders. The plight of the dispossessed of their homeland for whatever reason, innocents suffering from the ravages of war, and of course, the list goes on as we see this on the nightly news.

Secondly, try to be the best version of yourself you can be. Explore your talents, gifts, and abilities and develop these to their potential. If you can, continue to learn and grow, undertake, and continue studying, reading, and reflecting. The author believes this learning, including character development, carries you into the afterlife.

Thirdly, invest in your spiritual development as much as you invest in other segments of your life, such as family, hobbies, sports, and friends. Despite all the flaws and false teaching of some religions, they provide the opportunity to congregate in prayer, contemplate the wonderment of the unseen, and instill good values and morals in our children and society in general. Putting aside the misdirected dogma of the world's great religions (all claiming to be the only path to Heaven), they mostly teach sound principles and values of love, self-sacrifice, and compassion. The religiosity of prayer, singing of hymns, and reading from their Holy texts are all conducive to spiritual development. Many religions are rich in culture to instill self-sacrificing, whether fasting or participating in Holy Days and Religious Festivals. There are many ways to praise and glorify God and enrich one's spirituality.

In short, assisting the needs of others will provide the opportunity for service, which is reciprocated by the sense of purpose demonstrated in the offering – i.e., giving a purpose in life! The more you can give of yourself, the greater the joy and satisfaction which will be yielded.

The author trusts you will enjoy the remaining chapters of this book and draw enduring value.

Sources :

1. https://link.springer.com/article/10.1007/BF02229062

2. https://link.springer.com/article/10.1023/A:1009691405299

3. https://link.springer.com/article/10.1007/s11205-011-9863-0

4. https://plato.stanford.edu/entries/moral-arguments-god/

5. https://www.ncbi.nlm.nih.gov/pmc/articles/PMC4241367/

6. https://www.cambridge.org/core/journals/cambridge-quarterly-of-healthcare-ethics/article/germline-modification-and-the-burden-of-human-existence/167CB3680FE40EBE94FEF1E7B1978A02

7. https://www.sciencedirect.com/science/article/pii/0191886988901572

8. https://scholar.csl.edu/ctm/vol34/iss1/27/

9. https://www.tandfonline.com/doi/abs/10.1080/14746700.2015.1023525

10. https://digitalcommons.cedarville.edu/christian_engineering_conference/2017/calling_and_engineering/2/

11. https://digitalcommons.liberty.edu/honors/171/

12. http://www.cbfa-cbar.org/index.php/jbib/article/view/14

13. The Ra Material, Book, L & L Research

14. The Golden Dawn, Israel Regardie

15. The Book of Secret Wisdom

16. Mystic Qabalah, Dion Fortune

17. "Man's Search for Meaning" by Viktor Frank

18. "The Republic" by Plato" The Tao Te Ching by Lao Tzu

19. "American Psychological Association: https://www.apa.org/topics/life-meaning

Further Recommended Reading :

- "Existentialism and Humanism" by Jean-Paul Sartre
- "Thus Spoke Zarathustra" by Friedrich Nietzsche
- "The Oxford Handbook of Philosophy of Death" edited by John Martin Fischer
- "The Stoics" by F.H. Sandbach
- "The Essential Stoics: Selections from the Stoics," edited by L.C. Becker and Charlotte Becker
- "Nihilism: A Philosophical Essay" by Julian Young.
- "The Oxford Handbook of Philosophy of Death" edited by John Martin Fischer
- "The Meaning of Life" edited by E.D. Klemke
- "Existentialism is a Humanism" by Jean-Paul Sartre
- "Thus Spoke Zarathustra" by Friedrich Nietzsche
- "The Tao Te Ching" by Lao Tzu
- "The Bhagavad Gita"
- "The Bible"
- "The Quran"

Life After Death

— OUR JOURNEY CONTINUES... —

Chapter 3:

EXPLORING THE CONCEPT OF HEAVEN AND HELL: ARE THEY REAL OR MYTHICAL?

Heaven and Hell have been described and discussed in various religious and philosophical traditions throughout history. In Christianity, Heaven is often described as a place of eternal bliss and joy, and Hell is a place of eternal suffering and punishment. In Islam, Heaven (Jannah) and Hell (Jahannam) are also mentioned in the Quran and Hadith as the ultimate destination for individuals after death, based on their actions and beliefs during their lifetime. Also, in Hinduism, Hindu scriptures such as the Bhagavad Gita and the Puranas describe the concepts of Heaven (Swarga) and Hell (Naraka).

These are only a few examples, as Heaven and Hell can vary greatly between religious and philosophical traditions. It's important to note that these concepts are often based on faith and belief, and their existence has yet to be scientifically proven. It's important to note that opinion in Heaven and Hell is highly subjective and can vary greatly among individuals. According to surveys and studies, a large portion of the global population holds religious beliefs that include the existence of Heaven and Hell. For example, Christianity is the largest religion in the world, and most Christians believe in the existence of Heaven and Hell. However, not all people hold religious beliefs, and some may not believe in Heaven and Hell. Atheism, agnosticism, and various philosophical beliefs can all lead individuals to reject the idea of an afterlife and the existence of these concepts.

Where Do The Words "Heaven" And "Hell" Come From ?

The words "Heaven" and "Hell" have held a pivotal position in the Christian tradition for centuries, and theologians and writers have utilized their power to evoke both fears and hope for many years. The Christian version of Heaven and Hell arises from the doctrine of the Trinity [2], which states that God is a trinity of persons who exist in an eternal relationship of love. This doctrine gives a distinct shape to how Christians conceptualize Heaven and Hell : the essence of Heaven is a perfected relationship of love with the Trinitarian God that fulfills our nature. At the same time, Hell is the loss of this relationship and all the good things we were created for [2]. The prospects for happiness and misery are so magnified in the Christian doctrine that the meaning of our lives and the significance of our choices are both elevated to dramatic proportions [2]. Of course, other great theistic religions, such as Judaism and Islam, have their doctrines of salvation and corresponding accounts of Heaven and Hell [2]. C. S. Lewis' Heaven and Hell remains one of the fascinating accounts of the visionary experience ever written [1]. The truth was never so beautiful, nor the stakes ever so high, in the quest to find and follow the truth regarding Heaven and Hell [2]. The eternal joy of unimaginable glory and delight could be gained, and eternal misery of unspeakable horror could be suffered through Heaven or Hell [2].

Beliefs about supernatural punishment and the afterlife have been studied extensively concerning their effects on human cooperation [3]. Thoughts about God and the afterlife are powerful tools for motivating collaboration, as they invoke the threat of punishment for transgressions [3]. For example, research has found that beliefs about God lead to stronger thoughts about the unjustifiability of moral transgressions [3]. Furthermore, those who profess faith in heaven and hell and those who believe in a personal God will have stronger beliefs about the unjustifiability of moral transgressions [3]. As such, believers have been found to rate moral transgressions as less justifiable than non-believers [3].

Moreover, it has been suggested that people strategically endorse supernatural punishment beliefs as intuitive tools of social control to manipulate others into cooperating and that supernatural monitoring can activate cognitive architecture associated with reputation management and promote prosocial behavior [3]. It is also believed that various cognitive biases can compel the appeal to intuitions about immanent justice. Signaling one's trustworthiness through possessing supernatural punishment beliefs can also lead to increased cooperation [3]. Thus, it appears that beliefs about the afterlife [4], God, supernatural policing, and morality [3] are inextricably linked to the human need to cooperate and maintain social order.

Many world religions have similar concepts, and the cognitive science of religion (CSR) provides a theoretical framework for understanding how these beliefs emerge and are transmitted [5]. For example, many religions believe that good deeds are rewarded, and bad deeds are punished [5], known as the doctrine of Purgatory. This belief is likely the result of a cognitive tendency to think in terms of proportionality and a cognitive bias toward anthropomorphism [5]. This is evident in Islamic theology, which uses the works of al-Ghazālī as a basis for understanding the cognitive science of religion [5]. Studies have also shown that beliefs in the Balance doctrine are common among Muslim youth [5], further proving that the cognitive science of religion is a useful tool for understanding the emergence and transmission of religious beliefs. Additionally, CSR can be used to explain the prevalence of common religious beliefs such as reincarnation, trust in the power of dead ancestors, and faith in a personal destiny after death that precedes heaven [5]. Other religions also have similar concepts;

for example, the Buddhist religion teaches three levels of existence, and the Hindu religion teaches that there are two types of people [5]. By understanding the cognitive tendencies that play a role in the emergence and transmission of religious beliefs, we can gain a deeper understanding of religious phenomena [5].

Heaven and Hell have been around for centuries, with the idea of eternal bliss or misery providing moral and spiritual orientation for Western culture [2]. The Christian view of Heaven and Hell is that they are both part of the same process, with the ultimate destiny of everyone being determined by the choices they make in life [6]. This notion is based on the idea that God has granted us free will, and therefore we are responsible for our actions [6]. The implications of this are profound, as it means that God is not responsible for our choices, nor can He be held accountable for the difference between those who are saved and those who are not [6]. Furthermore, the Bible and other primary sources provide little information on what Heaven will be like, and theologians rarely offer specifics [6]. The only certainty is that there will be a final and irrevocable division within humanity, with some ending up in Heaven and others ending up in Hell [6]. As evidenced by the works of John Calvin and Arminius, the debate over what determines a person's destination has been ongoing for centuries [6]. Ultimately, it is possible that the terrible price of filling Heaven is also the filling of Hell and that in any other feasible world, God would have had to accept a worse balance between saved and lost [6]. Therefore, the evidence for Heaven and Hell is spiritual but also rational and philosophical [6], as they provide meaning and significance to our lives and choices [2].

The Origin, Meaning, And History Of The Word Hell

The word "Hell" has its origins in Old English, where it was spelled "hel" or "helle" and meant "the place of the dead." In Norse mythology, Hel was also the name of the underworld goddess.

Over time, the word "Hell" came to be associated with a place of eternal punishment and suffering for sinners in Christian theology. This concept of Hell is often depicted as a fiery pit or lake of fire where demons torment the souls of the damned.

The idea of Hell has a long history in religious and cultural traditions. In many cultures, the underworld was seen as a place of darkness and suffering. The ancient Egyptians, Greeks, and Romans all had myths and beliefs about an afterlife, which included ideas about punishment and reward.

In the Bible, Hell is sometimes called Sheol or Hades, the Jewish and Greek terms for the underworld. The concept of Hell as a place of punishment for the wicked developed in Christian theology and was heavily influenced by the writings of Dante Alighieri in the Divine Comedy, which popularized the idea of Hell as a hierarchical realm of punishment.

What Sciences Can Be Used To Prove That Heaven And Hell Exist?

One must first understand the underlying science to prove that Heaven and Hell exist. Dostoevsky's illuminating and influential writings, Heaven and Hell [7], remain a fascinating account of the most visionary experience ever written. In its sequel, the author explores the history and nature of mysticism [7]. Moreover, the Humanities [8] and the arts, particularly the art of poetry and the relationship between the artist and society [10], provide insight into the nature of human experience. William Blake's Marriage of Heaven and Hell [10] is a text that can easily be misinterpreted, and this is primarily due to its register and tone. Blake has written a text in which what appears to be mystical insight may blind the reader to a misunderstanding of its major themes [10]. Chaos Theory [8] is also a science that can be used to prove the existence of Heaven and Hell. Stanislaw Ulam's analogy of a chaotic machine [9] comes from Ian Stewart's book Does God Play Dice? The New Mathematics of Chaos [9] discusses the relationship between the two. Additionally, the laws of thermodynamics indicate that all energy is conserved, so energy can only be created or destroyed. Thus, these sciences provide evidence that Heaven and Hell exist. Other evidence, such as the research of Professor Bart Ehrman and findings reported in his book *Heaven and Hell - A History of the Afterlife,* suggests otherwise.

Do People Believe In Heaven And Hell?

Heaven and Hell have been part of the Christian tradition for centuries, with many people believing that good people go to Heaven and bad people go to Hell [6]. It is thought that Heaven is a deserved reward for a virtuous life, whereas Hell is a just punishment for a sinful life [6]. According to a common view in the wider Christian culture, Heaven and Hell compensate for our earthly lives [6]. Anselm speculated that if finite-duration suffering would not satisfy the demands of justice, perhaps suffering of infinite duration would do the trick [6]. However, many people reject a retributive theory of punishment, believing that no punishment can adequately compensate for the slightest offense against God [6]. Critics further argue that no suffering or sentence of any duration could ever pay for someone's wrongdoing, as punishment does nothing to cancel out sin, to compensate or make up for it, to repair the harm that it brings into our lives, or to heal the estrangement that makes it possible in the first place [6].

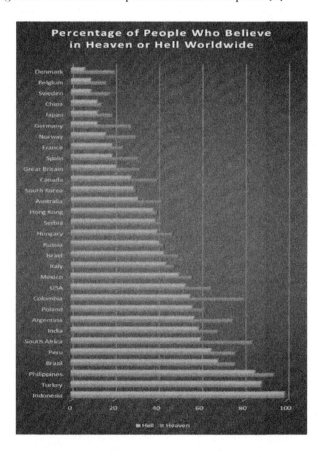

Source :

"Most Americans Believe in Heaven & Hell." Pew Research Center, Washington, D.C.,
https://www.pewresearch.org/fact-tank/2015/11/10/most-americans-believe-in-heaven-and-hell/

Christianity - When Did the Terms Heaven and Hell

The terms "Heaven" and "Hell" have been used in Christian theology for many centuries, and their origins can be traced back to the early years of the Christian Church.

Heaven, as a place of eternal happiness and bliss, can be found in the New Testament of the Christian Bible, particularly in the writings of the Apostle Paul. In the book of Revelation, the concept of Heaven is also described in detail, with a vision of a heavenly city and the throne of God. Similarly, the concept of Hell as a place of eternal punishment and suffering can also be found in the New Testament. In the Gospel of Matthew, Jesus warns of the "eternal fire" that awaits the wicked, and in the book of Revelation, Hell is depicted as a lake of fire and brimstone.

These terms became more widespread and codified as Christian theology developed over time. In the 4th century, theologians such as Augustine of Hippo and John Chrysostom wrote extensively about Heaven and Hell. Their teachings helped establish the doctrine of eternal punishment and reward in Christian theology.

Proof That Heaven And Hell Exist Using Scientific Evidence.

The existence of Heaven and Hell has remained a source of contention for centuries. While many subscribe to the notion that these two spiritual realms are real, no scientific evidence supports this belief. D.H. Lawrence wrote Heaven and Hell to explore this concept  scientifically [11]. In this book, he sought to uncover the history and nature of mysticism [11] but failed to provide any conclusive evidence that Heaven and Hell are real. Despite his efforts, the debate over their existence rages on, and scientific evidence has yet to be found.

Since the dawn of civilization, humanity has sought to understand and explain the world around it. Ancient philosophers and religious texts provide the earliest evidence of humanity's attempts to make sense of the world. Many documents, such as the Bible and the Vedas, reference concepts like love, justice, and morality. These ideas have been around for thousands of years and have been accepted by many cultures as fundamental truths. However, it is only in the last century that these concepts have been studied in a scientific context. Through research, scientists have proven that many of these concepts have a biological basis. For example, studies have shown that love is associated with releasing oxytocin in the brain. Similarly, the idea of justice has been linked to the activity of certain brain regions. This research helps to prove that these concepts have a long history and can be traced back to some of the earliest documents ever written. These studies demonstrate that these concepts have an objective, biological basis and are not just subjective beliefs. For example, in the past decade, shamanic figures have been studied in Japan [12], providing a unique insight into the supernatural world.

The Question Of Karma

Karma is a foundational principle of many Eastern religions, particularly Hinduism and Buddhism. The word karma was derived from the Sanskrit verb "kri," meaning "to act" [15], and can refer to both the actions and the consequences of the activities [16]. This spiritual concept of cause and effect is based on the idea that a person's intentional actions [14], whether positive or negative, will affect their future [16]. For example, positive actions create good karma, which leads to future happiness, while negative ones create bad karma [15], which leads to suffering.

Furthermore, in these spiritual traditions, karma is an ethical concept that guides the behavior of adherents and helps explain the inequalities in the world [19] [20]. Karma is closely associated with reincarnation, wherein the quality of one's current life is determined by the choices and actions of their past life [14]. In Hinduism, karma is closely related to the Vedas, ancient Hindu scriptures that teach that the choices and actions of an individual will shape the quality of their future [18]. This is more fully explored in Chapter 4.

The cause-and-effect cycle is further understood in the Hindu religion as the law of karma or the karma theory [14]. Buddhism also considers karma a cornerstone of spiritual growth, as it encourages people to be mindful of their actions [13]. Karma is often misunderstood and used loosely [13], but its true definition is rooted in intentional action [14]. We are all creating karma every minute, and the energy of our actions affects us every minute [16]. The rewards or retribution that follow karma are like a shadow that follows a person; this concept is even relevant in Taoism [14]. By understanding karma's literal definition, we can create positive outcomes for ourselves and others [13].

In short, the doctrine of karma implies that one person's karma cannot affect another person's future. Yet, many believe pious activities like pilgrimages can benefit living or deceased relatives [17]. Ultimately, karma is a universal principle of action and reaction, cause and effect, and it is believed to rule all consciousness [18].

Moreover, Karma is also an important concept in religion and philosophy. It is the notion that a person's actions and deeds will affect their present and future life [16]. The idea of cause and effect is deeply embedded in the concept of karma, which implies that one will receive the consequences of their actions [16] [19] [22]. The rules of karma apply to words and thoughts as well as actions [19], and the effect of one's actions may be felt in the present or the future [23]. In addition, karma does not merely punish or reward people but is instead a way of understanding cause and effect [22]. This cause-and-effect cycle is so powerful that it cannot be avoided, evaded, or cheated [23], and it is the energy that results from a person's actions [22]. Karma is a dynamic spiritual cycle of actions and consequences we control through our decisions and activities [16]. Furthermore, karma can manifest itself in a positive or negative form at any given moment, and it flows in a cycle throughout our lifetimes, generally lasting for 12 years [22]. Thus, we can use karma to our advantage by creating positive choices and thoughts, bringing about positive outcomes [16]. On the other hand, negative actions will lead to negative effects [21], such as suffering from the negative karmic effects of cheating on one's spouse [22].

What Is The Origin And Meaning Of The Word Satan

The word "Satan" comes from the Hebrew word "Satan" (שָׂטָן), which means "adversary" or "accuser." In Jewish and Christian traditions, Satan is a supernatural being often portrayed as an enemy of God and a tempter of humanity.

In the Hebrew Bible, "Satan" is used as a noun to describe a human opponent or adversary and as a verb to describe the act of opposing or obstructing someone. In the Book of Job, Satan appears as a divine prosecutor who challenges the righteousness of Job, causing God to allow him to test Job's faith.

In later Jewish and Christian traditions, Satan became associated with the fallen angel who rebelled against God and was cast out of heaven. He is often depicted as the embodiment of evil and the enemy of God and humanity.

The word "Satan" has also been used to refer to any force or entity that opposes or obstructs someone or something, such as a person's inner demons or societal oppression.

Understanding The Nature Of Evil, Satan, And Demons

The belief in evil, Satan, and demons are powerful and enduring phenomenon woven into religious and spiritual stories for centuries. These spiritual creatures are allegedly supernatural beings in the spiritual world, portrayed as evil and demonic [25] [24].

Demons are reported as powerful spirits that can possess people and cause them to act out the desires of demons [25]. In addition, demons are often said to be fallen angels who are superiors in authority [25]. Furthermore, it is claimed that the Devil, Satan, and demons are spirits that tempt people to sin and cause them to commit evil acts [25] [24]. They are powerful supernatural beings that tempt humans to sin and oppose God's authority [24]. Moreover, the devil or Satan, and demons are evil and dangerous [26] and are portrayed as threatening people or animals [24]. Although **fictional characters** from religious texts [24] remain in the collective consciousness and continue to haunt our imagination *(authors comment - perhaps left to frighten followers to observance in a particular religion, faith or following).*

Author's Comments

69

As a society, we have been badly duped by most large religions that use the fear factor of "going to Hell" as either recruitment or retention into their brand of religion. As children, we were like lambs to the slaughter in shaping our belief system, frightened about going to Hell and joining a religious group (generally that of our parents) to save our souls. The myth of their being an actual literal Hell can carry on into adulthood. Interestingly, each major religion points the way to Heaven as being (in most cases) exclusively through their belief system. Interestingly, most major and smaller religions preach and have part of their common teaching that if you don't make it to Heaven – you are going to an infernal Hell (possibly through Purgatory).

The author recognizes that some readers will cite the Holy Bible (and other Holy texts) that entry into Heaven or Paradise is through observance of their requirements and religious sacraments.

Distinguished Professor of Religious Studies at the University of North Carolina, Bart D. Ehrman, has revealed and reports in his extensive studies of ancient texts in his book "*Heaven and Hell – A History of the Afterlife*" some striking findings. These are paraphrased below and with thanks to Professor Ehrman for being allowed to share and cite the following :

"*My scholarship led me to realize that the Bible was a very human book, with human mistakes, biases, and culturally conditioned views. And realizing that made me wonder if the beliefs in God and Christ I had held and urged on others were partially biased, culturally conditioned, or even mistaken*". (Ehrman, 2020: xiv).

"*I was hearing, and starting to think, that the Bible was not a consistent revelation whose very words came from God; that the traditional doctrines I had always held as obviously true (e.g., the Trinity) were not handed down from heaven but were formulations made by very fallible human beings; and that there were lots of other views out there – even Christian beliefs – that did not jibe with what I had long believed (Ehrman, loc cit, xv)."*

"I'm saying that the ideas of heaven and hell were invented and altered over the years" (Ehrman, loc cit, xvii). *[Ed. Bold emphasis added by this book's author].*

This author is neither qualified to question nor challenge the research findings and efficacy of translation of ancient scriptures and, like other lay people, relies on the interpretation by scholars (like Professor Ehrman and Professor Scott Bruce, among many others) who have dedicated their lives to researching the 'truth' and publishing their findings through refereed scholarly journals.

It is the view of this author that, for the most part, the records and life of Jesus in the gospels are faithfully recorded and are, for the most part, accurate ; however, it is also apparent that loving and devout followers of Jesus when compiling the gospels would have been unable to provide unbiased and objective views, including reporting hearsay evidence. This leads to the final compilation being influenced beyond accurate observation, prone to exaggeration, and influenced by contemporary thoughts and values.

This presents a range of implications for deeper consideration. While today's devotees may draw comfort, for the most part, what is recorded is a reliable historical depiction of events that took place and satisfies at a 'his-story' level. In the author's view, it respectfully fails to meet the higher standard of acceptance *in toto* of the gospels being complete 'literal' truth.

The Bible has been made up of selective ancient texts to make up the Gospels of the New Testament. Other books, scrolls, and parchments have been rejected ; for example, the Gospel of Thomas, discovered in Egypt in 1945, was reportedly dismissed based on its narrative construct (although containing 114 sayings attributed to the resurrected Jesus) not fitting into the consistency of the final gospels selected. And the Book of Mary was rejected

71

as it was perhaps deemed unorthodox by the men who shaped the nascent Catholic Church and wished to downplay the contribution of women's contributions to the early Christian movement. For centuries Mary Magdalene was denigrated as a prostitute (or woman of loose morals), perhaps as a way of underplaying the significance of her contribution.

This process suggests only including evidence that supports the desired tenet of the Gospels of the New Testament.

Drawing on his background as an academic in commercial law, the author suggests he can assert some modest contribution in evaluating the reliability of documents through their provenance, a skill he possesses. When it comes to the gospels, it is widely acknowledged that they were recorded sometime after the events of Jesus and that multiple followers completed them at different times. This raises questions about the gospels' truth, total accuracy, and completeness, as their veracity (and acceptance of literality by Christians) depends solely on divine providence. Without the guiding hand of God, the gospels alone do not appear to be fully verifiable, making it difficult to argue that they should be taken as a literal record rather than a lyrical one. It is important to acknowledge that while the Bible's contents are mighty and its message beautiful and profound, it cannot be verified and must be considered within this limitation. This does not diminish the Bible's value as a source of joy and guidance for millions for centuries. To ensure its sustainability for future generations, it must be recognized for what it is - and its limitations respected.

References And Sources

1. Origin of the concepts of Heaven and Hell: Where do the words "Heaven" and "Hell" come from? Retrieved from *//books.google.com/books?hl=en&lr=&id=h5mMb-Jbxq4C&oi=fnd&pg=PT2&dq=Origin+of+the+concepts+of+Heaven+and+Hell+Where+do+the+words+%22Heaven%22+and+%22Hell%22+come+from%3F&ots=V2twwCOOtr&sig=ET4lVdPIgTXFToSQegUrDWLywss*

2. Heaven and Hell (Chapter) by Jerry Walls Retrieved from *https://www.taylorfrancis.com/chapters/edit/10.4324/9780203879344-68/heaven-hell-jerry-walls*

3. The Science of Heaven and Hell: Exploring the Origins and Meanings of the Concepts Retrieved from *https://www.sciencedirect.com/ science/article/pii/ S1090513810000899*

4. Tracing the History of Heaven and Hell: A Comparative Study Retrieved from *https://journal.fi/scripta/article/view/67154*

5. Heaven and Hell: Cultural and Philosophical Perspectives Retrieved from *https://www.mdpi.com/1369678*

6. Heaven and Hell: A Philosophical Inquiry Retrieved from *http://seop.illc.uva.nl/entries/heaven-hell/*

7. Do Heaven and Hell Exist? What Sciences Can Be Used to Prove Their Existence? Retrieved from *https://books.google.com/books?hl=en&lr=&id=h5mMb-Jbxq4C&oi=fnd&pg=PT2&dq=Does+Heaven+and+Hell+exist%3F+What+sciences+can+be+used+to+prove+Heaven+and+Hell+exist%3F&ots=V2twwCOOtt&sig=EP0Z2WsWICicRkhru_hAbenRG9s*

8. Humanities and Chaos Theory: A Response to Steenburg's "Chaos at the Marriage of Heaven and Hell" Retrieved from *https://www.cambridge.org/core/journals/harvard-theological-review/article/humanities-and-chaos-theory-a-response-to-steenburgs-chaos-at-the-marriage-of-heaven-and-hell/6DD0A26252F8933199C56387F455E37C*

9. Chaos at the Marriage of Heaven and Hell: A Critical Analysis Retrieved from *https://www.cambridge.org/core/journals/harvard-theological-review/article/chaos-at-the-marriage-of-heaven-and-hell/48BD91A69B1D4DBC66FD5A69D7A67C16*

10. Proving the Existence of Heaven and Hell: A Scientific Approach Retrieved from *https://digilib.phil.muni.cz/handle/11222.digilib/142612*

11. Proving Heaven and Hell Exists: Utilizing Scientific Evidence Retrieved from *https://books.google.com/books?hl=en&lr=&id=h5mMb-Jbxq4C&oi=fnd&pg=PT2&dq=Proving+Heaven+and+Hell+exists+How+can*

+we+prove+Heaven+and+Hell+exists+using+scientific+evidence%3F&ots=V2twwCOOss&sig=5SQspD1cYvHZe6F0qo17WcJtPBw

12. Blacker, Carmen. The Catalpa Bow: A Study of Shamanistic Practices in Japan. Taylor & Francis, 2000 Retrieved from https://www.taylorfrancis.com/books/mono/10.4324/9780203347133/catalpa-bow-carmen-blacker

13. "Definition and Theory of Karma." Dada Bhagwan Spiritual Articles. Retrieved from https://www.dadabhagwan.org/books-media/spiritual-articles/definition-and-theory-of-karma/

14. "Karma." Wikipedia. Retrieved from https://en.wikipedia.org/wiki/Karma

15. "Karma." Yogapedia. Retrieved from https://www.yogapedia.com/definition/4980/karma

16. "Here's a Great Explanation of What Karma Means and How You Can Improve Your Life." Ideapod. Retrieved from https://ideapod.com/heres-great-explanation-karma-really-means-can-improve-life/

17. "Karma." Encyclopaedia Britannica. Retrieved from https://www.britannica.com/topic/karma#:~:text=karma%2C%20Sanskrit%20karman%20(%E2%80%9Cact,modes%20of%20an%20individual's%20existence.

18. "Karma." The Original Buddhas. Retrieved from https://www.originalbuddhas.com/blog/karma

19. "What Is Karma?" Live Science. Retrieved from https://www.livescience.com/41462-what-is-karma.html

20. "How Karma Works." HowStuffWorks. Retrieved from https://people.howstuffworks.com/karma.htm

21. "What Is Karma?" WebMD. They were retrieved from https://www.webmd.com/balance/what-is-karma#:~:text=Hinduism%20identifies%20karma%20as%20the,cause%20and%20effect%20in%20morality.

22. Emoha.com. (n.d.). How Does Karma Impact Your Life? Retrieved from https://emoha.com/blogs/learn/how-does-karma-impact-your-life

23. The Pioneer. (2020). Karma - The Law of Cause and Effect. Retrieved from https://www.dailypioneer.com/2020/state-editions/karma---the-law-of-cause-and-effect.html

24. SHS Web of Conferences. (2018). Karma and Destiny: A Socio-Cultural Study of the Sikh Community in Malaysia. Retrieved from https://www.shsconferences.org/articles/shsconf/abs/2018/11/shsconf_cildiah2018_01119/shsconf_cildiah2018_01119.html

25. Google Books. (n.d.). Definition and Description: What are some characteristics of the Devil, Satan, and demons? Retrieved from https://books.google.com/books?hl=en&lr=&id=9160AH4UK1gC&oi=fnd&

*pg=PR15&dq=Definition+and+Description+What+are+some+characteristics +of+the+Devil,+Satan+and+demons%3F&ots=eE0KKPGjlz&sig=hGNK2HG LCh2WA60Q3-HXgNXS5xM**

26. Taylor & Francis. (n.d.). Folk Devils and Moral Panics. Retrieved from *https://www.taylorfrancis.com/books/mono/10.4324/9780203828250/folk-devils-moral-panics-stanley-cohen*

OTHERS SOURCES

27. *https://www.taylorfrancis.com/books/mono/10.4324/9781315002385/diction ary-gods-goddesses-devils-demons-manfred-lurker*
28. *https://www.emerald.com/insight/content/doi/10.1108/LHT-08-2014-0081/full/html*
29. *https://www.sciencedirect.com/science/article/pii/S8756328212013245*
30. *https://link.springer.com/article/10.1007/s10676-006-9111-5*
31. *https://www.sciencedirect.com/science/article/pii/S0885392403005165*
32. The Hebrew Bible (including the Book of Job)
33. The New Testament of the Christian Bible
34. Jewish and Christian commentaries and interpretations of religious texts
35. Academic Studies of Religion and Mythology

FURTHER READINGS

36. Hell: An Illustrated History of the Netherworld by Richard Craze
37. The Bible (particularly the New Testament book of Revelation)
38. The Divine Comedy by Dante Alighieri
39. The Encyclopedia of Christianity by Erwin Fahlbusch et al.
40. The Encyclopedia of Hell by Miriam Van Scott
41. The Summa Theological by Thomas Aquinas
42. The writings of early Christian theologians, such as Augustine of Hippo and John Chrysostom

Life After Death

— OUR JOURNEY CONTINUES... —

Chapter 4

REINCARNATION

Definition

Reincarnation is a concept that denotes the rebirth of a soul or spirit into a new body after death. It is a belief system that has existed for centuries and has its roots in many religions and cultures. Reincarnation is the transmigration of the soul from one body to another. The soul resides in a particular body due to karma or past actions. In the Hindu religion, reincarnation is an essential tenet, and it is believed that one's actions in their current life will determine their fate in the next life.

When 'that karma' is over, the soul leaves the body and is given another body, as 'new karma' under the supervision of God. The ancient Hindu script, "Bhagavad-gita" (sec 2. Cl. 23), compares this to a 'change of dress.'

"As a person puts on new garments, giving up old ones, the soul similarly accepts new material bodies, giving up the old and useless ones." Hindus believe rebirth is a fact, that the soul never dies even though the body parts.

The idea of rebirth after death is not exclusive to any specific culture or religion, as people from multiple backgrounds throughout history have embraced it. The concept of reincarnation is also prevalent in Buddhism, Jainism, Sikhism, and various indigenous religious systems worldwide. While the specifics of reincarnation may vary depending on the tradition or belief system, the idea of an afterlife and the continuation of the soul beyond physical death remains a central tenet for many worldwide [1]. However, Christianity does not acknowledge the phenomena of reincarnation in any way, shape, or form; pronouncing reincarnation does not exist, believing in an eternal soul instead of reincarnation citing Hebrews from the Bible: *"...it is appointed for man to die once, and after that comes judgment"* (Hebrews 9:27).

Despite the Christian view, the thought of reincarnation belongs to many other religions worldwide, including those which predate Christianity.

The Igbo people of Nigeria once held as a traditional part of their religion a belief of reincarnating back into families as a 'manner of speaking.' Akin to Western cultures where children resemble other family members, taking particular physical and behavioral features. However, this belief is now outdated and more prevalent with a traditionalist rather than in today's modern circles and unlikely to be recognized in the modern-day Igbo person. Moreover, traditional religion was more popular and had a much stronger foothold in pre-colonial Nigeria, noting that colonialism brought the Christian faith, which now occupies a strong foothold in the Nigerian 200 million population – with approximately 87 million people identifying as being Christian. It is also noted that earlier traditional reincarnation sentiments are not peculiar to just the Igbos but also to most cultural groups in Nigeria (and West Africa generally), including the Yourbas in Western Nigeria [2].

Roy W. Perrett [4] has argued that in Indian religions, the invoked rebirth type does not involve personal identity. In his article 'Rebirth,' he proposes that instead of a person being reborn, what is reborn is considered to be a "stream of consciousness" [4]. While the text suggests a philosophical argument favoring reincarnation by stating that one can continue to live in a disembodied form, it does not provide any specific philosophical arguments for or against reincarnation [4].

Reincarnation, as a concept, intersects with other beliefs about the afterlife in some cultures where it is widely accepted. According to studies, in areas where reincarnation is accepted, there are three forms of pre-natal and post-mortem identity: the continuing self/soul, the dissolution of the self, and family identity [5]. Family identity is a unique concept associated with reincarnation, implying that the soul is reborn into a close family member [5]. However, this understanding may be rare in Western cultures such as

Britain. In contemporary Western cultures, concepts similar to reincarnation may be labeled modern, postmodern, and kin-based [5]. People play with past identities and reincarnation in ways that cannot easily be reconciled with postmodern theories of the self. This is because these past identities strongly resemble current identities and may be considered part of the modernist project of the self [5].

In contrast, reincarnation is based on the belief that the soul continues to exist in different bodies. Rebirth and renewal are central to many religions and cultures worldwide. Therefore, while reincarnation may not be part of the beliefs about the afterlife in some cultures, it continues to be an important concept in others.

The mystery of reincarnation

One of the mysteries puzzling the human mind since the origin of humanity is the concept of "reincarnation," which means "to take on the flesh again." As the civilizations evolved, beliefs got discriminated against and disseminated into various religions. The major division manifested was "East" and "West." The Eastern faiths being more philosophical and less analytical, have accepted reincarnation. However, the different Eastern religions like Hinduism, Jainism, and Buddhism have differed in their belief in rebirth. Further, Islam, as well as the dominant religion of the world, Christianity, having its origin in the West, as mentioned, has largely denied reincarnation. However, some sub-sects still show interest in it. Also, many mystic and esoteric schools like theosophical society have their unique description of rebirth. This article describes reincarnation as perceived by various religions, new religious movements, and some research evidence.

HINDUISM

Hindus believe reincarnation occurs when the soul or spirit, after biological death, begins a new life in a new body that may be human, animal, or spiritual, depending on the moral quality of the previous life's actions. The universal process that gives rise to the cycle of death and rebirth, governed by karma, is called "Samsara." "Karma" is action, which may be good or bad. He chooses his subsequent birth based on the type of karma one does. For example, if one has done a lot of divine services and wants to do more favor at the time of death, his soul chooses a family that supports his desire for rebirth. According to Hinduism, even Devas (Gods) may die and be born again. But here, the term "reincarnation" is not strictly applicable. Lord Vishnu is known for his 10 incarnations – "Dasavataras."

In Hinduism, in the holy book Rigveda, the oldest extant Indo-Aryan text, numerous references are made to rebirths.

The Bhagavad Gita states: "Never was there a time when I did not exist, nor you, nor all these kings; nor in the future shall any of us cease to be. As the embodied soul continuously passes, in this body, from childhood to youth to old age, the soul similarly passes into another body at death.

JAINISM

Jainism is historically connected with the sramana tradition with which the earliest mentions of reincarnation are associated. In Jainism, the soul and matter are considered eternal, uncreated, and perpetual. There is a constant interplay between the two, resulting in bewildering cosmic manifestations in material, psychic and emotional spheres around us. This led to the theories of transmigration and rebirth. Changes but not a total annihilation of spirit and matter is the basic postulate of Jain philosophy.

After death, life as we know it now moves on to another form of life based on the merits and demerits it accumulated in its current life. The path to becoming a supreme soul is to practice non-violence and be truthful.

Karma forms a central and fundamental part of the Jain faith, intricately connected to other philosophical concepts like transmigration, reincarnation, liberation, non-violence (ahimsā), and non-attachment. Actions are seen to have consequences: Some immediate, some delayed, and even into future incarnations. The doctrine of karma is not considered about one lifetime but also future images and past lives. *"Karma is the root of birth and death. The souls bound by karma go round and round in the cycle of existence."* Whatever suffering or pleasure that a soul may be experiencing in its present life is on account of choices it has made in the past. As a result of this doctrine, Jainism attributes supreme importance to pure thinking and moral behavior.

The Jain texts postulate four gates, states-of-existence, or birth categories, within which the soul transmigrates. The four gates are Deva (demi-gods), manussya (humans), nāraki (hell beings), and tiryañca (animals, plants, and micro-organisms). The four gates have four corresponding realms or habitation levels in the vertically tiered Jain universe: Demi-gods occupy the higher levels where the heavens are situated; humans, plants, and animals occupy the middle classes; and hellish beings occupy the lower levels, where seven hells are situated. Depending on karma, a soul transmigrates and reincarnates within this cosmology of destinies. The four main fortunes are further divided into sub-categories and still smaller sub-categories. In all, Jain texts speak of a cycle of 8.4 million birth destinies in which souls find themselves repeatedly as they cycle within samsara.

81

In Jainism, God has no role to play in an individual's destiny; one's destiny is not seen because of any reward or punishment system but because of its karma. Violent deeds, killing of creatures having five sense organs, eating fish, and so on lead to rebirth in hell. Deception, fraud, and falsehood lead to rebirth in the animal and vegetable world. Kindness, compassion, and humble character result in human birth, while austerity and the making and keeping of vows lead to rebirth in heaven. Each soul is thus responsible for its predicament and its salvation.

BUDDHISM

The Buddhist concept of reincarnation differs from others in that there is no eternal "soul," "spirit," or "self" but only a "stream of consciousness" that links life with life. The actual process of change from one life to the next is called punarbhava (Sanskrit) or punabbhava (Pāli), literally "becoming again," or more briefly, bhava, "becoming." The early Buddhist texts discuss techniques for recalling previous births, predicated on developing high levels of meditative concentration.[15] Buddha reportedly warned that this experience could be misleading and should be interpreted carefully. He taught a distinct concept of rebirth constrained by the concepts of 'anattā' that there is no irreducible 'atman' or "self" tying these lives together, which contrasts with Hinduism, where everything is connected. In a sense, "everything is everything."

In Buddhist doctrine, the evolving consciousness (Pali: samvattanika-viññana) or stream of consciousness (Pali: viññana-system), upon death (or "the dissolution of the aggregates") becomes one of the contributing causes for the arising of a new aggregation. At the end of one personality, a new one comes into being, much as the flame of a dying candle can serve to light the love of another. The consciousness in the new person is neither identical to nor entirely different from that in the deceased but the two form a causal continuum or stream. Transmigration is the effect of karma (Pali: kamma) or volitional action. The basic cause is the abiding consciousness in ignorance (Pali: Avijja, Sanskrit: Avidya): When ignorance is uprooted, rebirth ceases.

Vipassana meditation uses "bare attention" to mind-states without interfering, owning, or judging. Observation reveals each moment as an experience of an individual mind-state, such as a thought, a memory, a feeling, or a perception that arises, exists, and ceases. This limits the power of desire, which, according to the second noble truth of Buddhism, is the cause of suffering (dukkha) and leads to Nirvana (Nibbana, vanishing [of the self-ideal]) in which self-oriented models are transcended and "the world stops." Thus, consciousness is a continuous birth and death of mind-states: Rebirth is the persistence of this process.

SIKHISM

Sikhism preaches the path of "Bhakti" to achieve salvation. Sikhs believe the soul is passed from one body to another until liberation. If we perform good deeds and actions and remember the creator, we attain a better life, while if we carry out evil actions and sinful acts, we will be incarnated into "lower" life forms. God may pardon wrongs and release us. Otherwise, reincarnation is due to the law of cause and effect but does not create any caste or differences among people.

ISLAM

Reincarnation is refuted by all the main monotheistic religions of the world. This is because it is against their basic teachings of a finite life for the human upon which they are judged and rewarded accordingly. If a human

83

goes through numerous lives, which life will they be judged on? The first life? The last life? Considering this, the Quran rejects the concept of reincarnation, though it preaches the existence of the soul. The principal belief in Islam is that there is only one birth on this earth. Doomsday comes after death, and one will be judged whether one must once and for all go to hell or be unified with God. However, a few Muslim sects accept reincarnation, particularly the Shia sect (Ghulat) and others in the Muslim world, such as Druzes. Ghulat Shia Muslim sect regards its founders as, in some special sense, divine incarnations (hull). Historically, South Asian Isma'ilis performed changes yearly, one of which is for sins committed in past lives. Further, Sinan ibn Salman ibn Muhammad, also known as Rashid al-Din Sinan, (r. 1162-92), subscribed to the transmigration of souls as a tenet of the Alawi, who is thought to have been influenced by Isma'ilism. Modern Sufis who embrace the idea of reincarnation include Bawa Muhaiyadeen.

JUDAISM

Reincarnation is not an essential tenet of traditional Judaism. It is not mentioned in the Tanakh ("Hebrew Bible"), the classical rabbinical works (Mishnah and Talmud), or Maimonides' 13 principles of Faith, though the tale of the Ten Martyrs in the Yom Kippur liturgy, whom Romans killed to atone for the souls of the 10 brothers of Joseph, is read in Ashkenazi Orthodox Jewish communities. Medieval Jewish Rationalist philosophers discussed the issue, often in rejection. However, Jewish mystical texts (the Kabbalah), from their classic Medieval canon onwards, teach a belief in Gilgul Neshamot (Hebrew for metempsychosis of souls: Literally "soul cycle"). Other Non-Hasidic, Orthodox Jewish groups, while not heavily emphasizing reincarnation, acknowledge it as a valid teaching. The 16th-century Isaac Luria (the Ari) brought the issue to the center of his new mystical articulation for the first time and advocated the identification of the reincarnations of historical Jewish figures that Haim Vital compiled in his Shaar HaGilgulim.

As mentioned earlier, the major Christian denominations reject the concept of reincarnation. Christians believe that when a person dies, their soul sleeps in the grave along with their corpse. This soul sleep continues until a time in the future known as the "last day," also known as the "final judgment." But there is evidence in the Bible of Jesus himself teaching reincarnation. However, there was a schism in understanding Jesus himself in early Christian history. Was he a man who became God? Was God born as a man? The struggle was between the Church established by Paul in Rome and the remnants of the Jerusalem Church who fled to Egypt after Rome invaded Israel in 70 AD. The Roman faction rejected pre-existence and reincarnation and believed Jesus was God to become a man. The Jerusalem faction knew Jesus was a man who achieved the human-divine-at-one-ment, which is the goal of everyone to escape the reincarnation cycle of birth and death and have eternal life. However, Rome won the political battle, and the orthodox definition of resurrection was reduced to an end-of-time "Night of the Living Dead."

However, the Christian sects such as the Bogomils and the Cathars, who professed reincarnation and other gnostic beliefs, were referred to as "Manichean" and are today sometimes described by scholars as "Neo-Manichean." Recent studies have indicated that some Westerners accept the idea of reincarnation, including certain contemporary Christians, modern Neopagans, followers of Spiritism, Theosophists, and students of esoteric philosophies such as Kabbalah. The belief in reincarnation is particularly firm in the Baltic countries, with Lithuania having the highest figure for Europe, 44%. In a survey by the Pew Forum in 2009, 24% of American

Christians believed in reincarnation. Geddes MacGregor, an Episcopalian priest who is an Emeritus Distinguished Professor of Philosophy at the University of Southern California, a Fellow of the Royal Society of Literature, a recipient of the California Literature Award (Gold Medal, non-fiction category), and the first holder of the Rufus Jones Chair in Philosophy and Religion at Bryn Mawr, demonstrates in his book *Reincarnation in Christianity: A New Vision of the Role of Rebirth in Christian Thought*, that Christian doctrine and reincarnation are not mutually exclusive belief systems.

New religious movements

A new religious movement (NRM) (earlier known as 'cult') is a religious community or ethical, spiritual, or philosophical group of modern and recent origin with a peripheral place within the dominant religious culture. NRMs may be novel in source or part of a wider religion, such as Christianity, Hinduism, or Buddhism, in which case they will be distinct from pre-existing denominations. Several such movements include the Theosophical Society, Eckankar, Scientology, Meher Baba, Sai Baba, Brahmakumaris, Osho, etc.

All spiritual schools accept the concept of reincarnation. They admit, with some differences, that the purpose of reincarnation is for the soul to get purified and gain wisdom so that it comes out of the cycle of birth and death. The only spiritual guru with a different explanation for reincarnation is "Osho." Osho, also known as Bhagavan Rajaneesh, says that life is born when existence looks upon itself. An individual is a consciousness localized in a body. An individual's mind exists as a set of good and bad memories. Commonly more bad memories than good ones, as most people always tend to remember insults and criticisms more than praises. Memory is nothing but energy in a very subtle form. Being a point, it cannot be destroyed even at death. It is liberated into the cosmos and dissolved. Just like riches attract more riches, such memories are pooled up, only to enter another womb. When a person is born, he gets memories from many people and cannot remember his birth. Nevertheless, in exceptional cases, when a newborn gets the entire memory system of another individual, they can easily recall past dawn, though it is not their birth. So, in the true sense, the person is not born again; only memories are expressed in another individual. An enlightened person is not born again as their mind contains no good or bad memories—one life in a moment-to-moment existence. One doesn't carry forward any memory of previous life, i.e., no importance is attached to any event in life. It is like the path of a fish in the water or a bird in the sky. They do not leave any tracks behind. When enlightened people die, they go no memories to be picked up by other beings believing they are not born again.

How many times does a spirit reincarnate?

Lord Buddha talked about the cycle of birth and death – where souls keep reincarnating until desires have been fulfilled or transcended. After death, some believe the soul leaves the body and remains in the soul's world. After some time, the soul takes a new incarnation in a new body. Reincarnation is necessary until one achieves our full God-realization. This means some transcend desires and identify with the ego but are aware of the Supreme Self. At this point, the soul can remain in the bliss of nirvana.

How many incarnations are necessary for a soul to attain the highest realization? For every soul, it is different, but the scriptures say it is countless times.

Studies

The concept of past lives or reincarnation is a topic of much debate and interest, and there have been several studies and theories proposed about it. Here are some sources that discuss past life theories and research findings:

This book by Dr. Ian Stevenson, psychiatrist, and researcher, presents his research into cases of children who claim to remember past lives. He examines the evidence for reincarnation and proposes that birthmarks and birth defects may be related to injuries sustained in a past life [6]. Stevenson's work is highly regarded by many in the scientific community; At the same time, some have criticized his methods and conclusions, while others have praised his rigor and dedication to investigating a phenomenon often dismissed by mainstream science.

The twenty cases presented in the book are considered the most convincing examples of reincarnation that Stevenson found during his research. Stevenson's research investigated cases worldwide, including in India, Sri Lanka, Thailand, and Turkey. In each case, he interviewed the child, their family, and anyone else who may have had information about the claimed past life. He also attempted to verify the details of the past life that the child reported, such as the names and locations of people and places from the past. Some topics he affirmed include a Burmese girl who claimed to remember being her grandmother in a previous life. A boy from India remembered being a man from a neighboring village whom a gunshot wound had killed. A boy from Turkey claimed to remember being a man his wife had killed with an axe, and a girl from Sri Lanka remembered being a young woman who had died of complications from childbirth.

His book includes detailed analyses of the evidence gathered by Stevenson. It compares the children's memories to the actual events that occurred in the past lives they claim to remember to then evaluates the accuracy and consistency of their statements. His research also compares the cultural contexts in which these cases occurred. He found that while there were differences in how reincarnation was conceptualized and discussed in different cultures, the basic idea of a soul or consciousness being reborn in a new body was a common belief in many societies.

One of the most striking aspects of Stevenson's research is the emotional impact of past-life memories on children and their families. In many cases, the children expressed a strong attachment to their previous families and homes and experienced a sense of loss and longing for their past lives. Some families even arranged to meet and reconcile with the families of their child's supposed past life.

While "*Twenty Cases Suggestive of Reincarnation*" does not offer definitive proof of the reality of reincarnation, it does provide compelling evidence that many people, especially children, believe they have lived past lives. Stevenson's careful documentation and analysis of these cases have been praised for 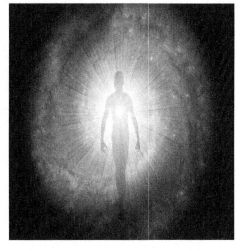 their scientific rigor and attention to detail. They continue to inspire further research into the mysteries of consciousness and the afterlife.

Stevenson's work has significantly impacted the study of consciousness and the nature of the self. His research challenges traditional Western views of the self as a fixed and continuous entity and suggests that consciousness may be more complex and fluid than previously thought. Stevenson's work has also interested those studying the relationship between memory and identity. The past-life memories of the children he looked at raise questions about how our memories shape our sense of self and our understanding of the world around us.

Critics of Stevenson's work have pointed out that there may be other explanations for the children's memories, such as suggestibility or cultural conditioning. However, as mentioned, Stevenson's methods and analyses have been praised for their rigor and attention to detail. He ruled out alternative explanations before concluding that the children's memories were evidence of reincarnation. In a later study by Stevenson I. (2003), he considers cases of individuals from Europe who claim to remember past lives. He examines the evidence for reincarnation and discusses the implications of his findings for a clearer understanding of consciousness and the nature of the self. [10]

Stevenson also published numerous other works on reincarnation and past-life memories. His work on reincarnation is a source of fascination and debate among those interested in reincarnation and the nature of consciousness. His research inspires new studies and discussions about the nature of consciousness and the afterlife. His legacy has helped to expand our understanding of what it means to be human.

Other researchers on reincarnation include the work of Dr. Jim B. Tucker, a psychiatrist at the University of Virginia, who presents his research into children who claim to remember past lives. He examines the evidence for reincarnation and discusses the implications of his findings. [7]

The Mills & Haraldsson study examines the experiences of individuals who claim to have memories of past lives. The authors discuss the characteristics of past-life experiences and propose that they may have therapeutic benefits. [8]

Shroder examines cases of children who claim to remember past lives and presents evidence for reincarnation. He also discusses the implications of past-life memories for our understanding of consciousness and the nature of the self. [9].

Other published findings on reincarnation

Case 1: The Reincarnation of Shanti Devi. [11]. Shanti Devi was born in Delhi, India, in 1926. At age four, she began to claim that her real home was in Mathura, a town over 100 miles away. She gave details of her past life, including her husband's name and occupation, her son's name, and the street on which she lived. Her statements were so detailed and specific that her parents decided to investigate. They traveled to Mathura, where they found a man who matched Shanti Devi's description of her husband. He confirmed many of the details she had given, including the street on which they had lived. Shanti Devi also recognized her son and identified her former home.

Case 2: The Reincarnation of Anne Frank. Hamer, J. (2009). Soul Survivor: The Reincarnation of a World War II Fighter Pilot. Grand Central Publishing.

91

James Leininger was born in Louisiana in 1998. From age two, he began to have nightmares about being a World War II fighter pilot named James Huston Jr. He would scream and thrash in his sleep, and his parents could not understand why. However, when James was three, he began to talk about his past life as a pilot. He gave details of his plane, his missions, and the name of his aircraft carrier. His parents were skeptical until they began to research the facts he had given. They discovered that there had indeed been a pilot named James Huston Jr. who had flown missions from the USS Natoma Bay. James Leininger's case was studied by Dr. Jim Tucker, who wrote about it in his book "*Return to Life: Extraordinary Cases of Children Who Remember Past Lives.*"

Case 3: *The Reincarnation of Lama Yeshe.* Coleman, G. (2005). The Autobiography of a Tibetan Monk. Wisdom Publications.

Lama Yeshe was a Tibetan Buddhist monk who died in 1984. Several years after his death, a young boy named Osel Hita Torres was born in Spain. When Osel was three, he began claiming he was Lama Yeshe. He gave detailed descriptions of the monastery where he had lived and the people who had surrounded him. His parents were skeptical, but they eventually took him to meet Lama Zopa Rinpoche, one of Lama Yeshe's closest disciples. Rinpoche was convinced that Osel was the reincarnation of Lama Yeshe and began to train him as a Buddhist monk. Osel spent several years in India studying with other monks and eventually became a respected teacher in his own right. His story is told in the book "The Autobiography of a Tibetan Monk" by Guy Newland.

Case 4: *The Reincarnation of Swarnlata Mishra.* Trivedi, S. (2008). Born Again: Reincarnation Cases Involving Evidence of Past Lives, with Xenoglossy Cases Researched by Ian Stevenson, MD. McFarland.

Swarnlata Mishra was born in 1948 in India. At the age of three, she began to speak of a previous life in a nearby village, claiming that she was a woman named Biya Pathak who had died giving birth to her son. Swarnlata provided detailed descriptions of Biya's life and family, including the names of her husband and children and specific events that had occurred in her life. She could also identify her previous home and others from her past life. Her statements were so accurate that her father decided to investigate. He traveled to the village and found Biya's family, who confirmed many of the details that Swarnlata had given.

Case 5: The Reincarnation of Ryan Hammons. Tucker, J. B. (2013).. *Return to Life: Extraordinary Cases of Children Who Remember Past Lives.* Macmillan.

Ryan Hammons was born in Oklahoma in 2005. At age four, he began talking about his past life as a Hollywood actor named Marty Martyn, who had starred in movies in the 1930s and 1940s. He gave detailed descriptions of Martyn's life and career, as well as his death at 61. Ryan's parents were skeptical, but they eventually began to research the details that he had given. They discovered that there had indeed been an actor named Marty Martyn, who had appeared in several movies during the 1930s and 1940s before dying at 59. Ryan's case was studied by Dr. Jim Tucker, who included it in his book "Return to Life: Extraordinary Cases of Children Who Remember Past Lives."

Case 6: The Reincarnation of P.M. Narendra Gupta. Tucker, J. B. (2013). *Return to Life: Extraordinary Cases of Children Who Remember Past Lives.* Macmillan.

P.M. Narendra Gupta was a wealthy businessman from Delhi, India, who died in 1967. Several years later, a young boy named P.M.

Subramanian was born in the same city. When Subramanian was three years old, he began to talk about his past life as Gupta. He gave details of Gupta's business dealings, personal life, and family. Subramanian also recalled events after Gupta's death, such as the division of his estate and the resolution of a legal dispute. His case was investigated by his family and others, who confirmed many of the details that he had given. Subramanian eventually went on to become a successful businessman in his own right. His case was studied by Dr. Jim Tucker, who included it in his book *"Return to Life: Extraordinary Cases of Children Who Remember Past Lives."*

Case 7: The Reincarnation of James Leininger. Tucker, J. B. (2005). *Life Before Life: A Scientific Investigation of Children's Memories of Previous Lives.* St. Martin's Press. [12]

James Leininger was born in 1998 in Louisiana, USA. At age two, he began to have nightmares about being a pilot during World War II. He would scream "Jack Larsen" and "Natoma" in his sleep. James' parents eventually researched the names and discovered that a man named Jack Larsen had been a member of the US Navy in World War II and had served on a ship called the Natoma Bay. They also found that a pilot named James Huston Jr. had died in a battle over the Pacific Ocean and that many of the details James had given about his past life matched Huston's life. James' case was studied by Dr. Jim Tucker, who included it in his book *"Life Before Life: A Scientific Investigation of Children's Memories of Previous Lives."*

Case 8: The Reincarnation of Anne Frank. Keilson, H. (2001). *Comedy in a Minor Key.* Farrar, Straus, and Giroux.

Helga Weiss was born in 1929 in Prague, Czechoslovakia. During World War II, she and her family were sent to the Terezin concentration camp, where she kept a diary of her experiences. After the war, she moved to Switzerland and became a successful artist. In the 1980s, she felt strongly connected to Anne Frank and her diary. She even had dreams in which she was Anne Frank. Weiss eventually met with Otto Frank, Anne's father, who confirmed many details she had given about her past life. Weiss' case is not a classic example of reincarnation, but it does involve a strong sense of identification with Anne Frank's life and experiences.

Case 9: *The Reincarnation of Walter Semkiw.* Semkiw, W. (2011). Cited in Born Again: Reincarnation Cases Involving Evidence of Past Lives, with Xenoglossy Cases Researched by Ian Stevenson, MD. Trivium Publishing.

Walter Semkiw was born in Detroit, USA, in 1955. In his mid-thirties, he became interested in reincarnation and began researching the topic. He eventually discovered Dr. Ian Stevenson, who had studied cases of reincarnation for many years. Semkiw became convinced that he had been a reincarnation of Reinhard Heydrich, a high-ranking Nazi official assassinated during World War II. He claimed that many of the details of Heydrich's life matched his own, including his physical appearance and personality traits. Semkiw eventually wrote a book about his experiences and his belief in reincarnation. His case is controversial; some have criticized his research methods and conclusions.

The emergence of new age spirituality.

Since ancient times, an understanding of the unseen world has existed, explained by shamans, priests, and 'mystics.' Before the dominance of institutionalized religion, humanity's belief systems were various delineations of polytheism and philosophical contemplations.

Ironically, the modern phenomenon of New Age spirituality is not new. The contemporary form of an age-old spiritual understanding existed in some form under every Western empire. Following the dominance of the Roman Catholic Church and their notorious criminalization of paganistic activities, that which was formerly called philosophy and science was painted black and has ever since been recognized as the occult, meaning 'hidden.'

The origins of many occult explorations are, ironically, extremely invested in the spiritual traditions and symbols investigated by many institutionalized religions. The most prominent is Judaic mysticism and their mysterious and ancient system of perceiving the archetypical mind of God,

called the Mystic Kabbalah. Many renowned occultists dedicate their lives to understanding this system or diagram of existential philosophy, similar to those recognized and respected as Rabbis. A few famous contemporary occultists include Israel Regardie and Allistair Crowley, who have extensively discussed this system [13].

The study of mystic traditions and symbols used by orthodox religions has existed through mystery schools and secret societies for centuries. The most obscure is a complete enigma to those not considered members, who pass down understandings that they guard with the utmost care. These traditions have many guises, but in the West, they all emerge from a tradition understood as Hermeticism, which gains its wisdom from the so-called god Thoth-Hermes, who is fabled to have existed and given knowledge to both the Greeks and Egyptians about mystic understandings. Their wisdom is obtained from surviving Ancient Egyptian artifacts (18).

Before the culture of secrecy, the philosophers of ancient Greece openly explored metaphysical understanding and were considered academics and scholars for it. Many philosophers marveled at the wisdom of the Egyptians and studied under their priests; Plato was rumored to be one of them (18).

The famous scholar Pythagoras was one of the first known scientist-mystics in ancient Greece, who influenced the likes of Plato and Aristotle with teachings well known in the Magna Graecia. Western civilization, as we know it, was massively influenced by the teaching of this man and his disciples, and much of his religious teachings either correlate to or directly influence Hermetic mysticism. The same mysticism has been closely followed over the years by academic occultists seeking an understanding of the origins of our universe. Eventually, they would band together to form The Hermetic Order of the Golden Dawn—a world-renowned so-called 'magical order' (18).

One of Pythagoras' principal teachings was the numeric system's sacred nature. He believed deep philosophy existed in every number and its mathematical properties. This resonates with the Judaic Kabbalists who number all 10 stations in their sacred Tree of Life, recognizing each number and accommodating stations to hold secrets about the mysterious nature of creation (14).

What is life according to new age spirituality?

Those who believe in spirituality understand that the Universe, similar to the numeric system, is infinite by nature. God is, thus, unknowable through any sound system of understanding, just as one cannot hope ever to understand the entirety of the numeric system using reason or logic. The conclusive "infinity," which encompasses the whole of the numeric system,

97

and indeed the universe, holds the answer, which is philosophical or spiritual.

When discussing infinity, we must use our faculties of intuition. Indeed, the duality of necessity with both logic and intuition/emotion is significant. The meaning of life or experiences, in general, may only be gleaned by utilizing both faculties in conjunction. The numeric system articulates and expresses infinity. However, forever is from which the numeric system originated and is the entirety of it. We may apply this to our manifested universe. All of the manifestations of creation (including you and me) are expressions or articulations of an infinite source or God and may be encapsulated by this single principle. Infinity may also be considered to be the principle of Unity. It is everything yet one single thing (13).

This is completely different from the general belief in popular traditions that God stands separate and above the rest of his creation. This is an example of how we have, over the years, begun to personify this one thing, injecting it with personalities and various aspects, which is where historically, manufactured "gods" emerge to explain every phenomenon. Eventually, interestingly we have unified creation under a single god yet have personified him as an entity rather than the entirety of what has been called the "mighty fabric" by Thoth-Hermes (17).

Authors Comment

This author cannot give an informed opinion as to whether reincarnation occurs. While there are significant reported cases that dedicated researchers have scientifically verified, the evidence remains anecdotal. Compared to the enormous body of anecdotal evidence of near-death experiences, which in the author's view provides compelling 'proof' of its existence, compared to reincarnation, which requires greater research and examination. However, while not knowing of the veracity of reincarnation, this author would not be surprised if this occurs and respectfully feels it makes perfect sense for God to assist the ongoing spiritual development of souls in the afterlife who may benefit from rebirth. By the Grace of God, all things are possible, and this might include reincarnation. Studies and research into past lives tend to support this possibility.

References:

1. Should Psychotherapy Consider Reincarnation? The Journal of Nervous and Mental Disease.https://journals.lww.com/jonmd/FullText/2012/02000/Should_Psychotherapy_Consider_Reincarnation_.11.aspx Accessed 2023-03-12

2. The Belief in Reincarnation Among the Igbo of Nigeria1 in Journal of Asian and African Studies Volume 20 Issue 1-2 (1985).https://brill.com/view/journals/jaas/20/1-2/article-p13_2.xml Accessed 2023-03-12

3. The Thomist: A Speculative Quarterly Review.https://muse.jhu.edu/pub/16/article/637420/summary Accessed 2023-03-12

4. Reincarnation and Relativized Identity 1.https://www.cambridge.org/core/journals/religious-studies/article/reincarnation-and-relativized-identity1/773FAA581827F0A18971D9A5451D8A2E Accessed 2023-03-12

5. Reincarnation, Modernity, and Identity.https://www.cambridge.org/core/journals/sociology/article/reincarnation-modernity-and-identity/3889FFF0C7324A1017C03F6C8E2BE3FE Accessed 2023-03-12

6. Stevenson, I. (1997). Reincarnation and Biology: A contribution to the etiology of birthmarks and birth defects. Praeger Publishers.

7. Tucker, J. B. (2005). Life Before Life: A Scientific Investigation of Children's Memories of Previous Lives. St. Martin's Press.

8. Mills, A., & Haraldsson, E. (2017). The phenomena of past-life experiences: An exploratory study. Journal of Near-Death Studies, 35(1), 35-52.

9. Shroder, T. (2014). Old souls: Compelling evidence from children who remember past lives. Simon and Schuster.

10. Stevenson, I. (2003). European Cases of the Reincarnation Type. McFarland & Company.

11. Stevenson, I. (1980). Twenty Cases Suggestive of Reincarnation. Publisher: the University of Virginia Press.

12. Tucker J. B. (2005). The Reincarnation of James Leininger. St. Martin's Press.

13. The Ra Material, Book, L & L Research ᴧᴧ

14. The Golden Dawn, Israel Regardie https://archive.org/search.php?query=subject%3A%22Magie+Cer%C3%A9monielle%22

15. Dushkova, Z. (2015). The Book of Secret Wisdom: The Prophetic Record of Human Destiny & Evolution. Radiant Books,

16. Mystic Qabalah, Dion Fortune**

17. Asclepius: The Perfect Discourse of Hermes Trismegistus # #

18. The Seeker's Guide to The Secret Teachings of All Ages: The Authorized Companion to Manly P. Hall's Esoteric Landmark, Mitch Horowitz.

ᴧᴧ The Ra Material, or The Law of One, is a series of books written by Don Elkins, Carla Rueckert, and James McCarty and compiled by L & L Research. It is a channeled work that allegedly documents conversations between an entity known as Ra and the authors.

L & L Research is a non-profit organization founded to study the phenomenon of UFOs and extra-terrestrial intelligence, as well as metaphysical and spiritual topics. The Ra Material is one of their most well-known works and has been praised for its depth and complexity. The Ra Material teaches that all existence is one non-dualistic consciousness, that all individuals are connected, and that the ultimate goal is reuniting with this consciousness. The material also discusses the nature of time, the role of the human mind in spiritual evolution, and the principles of karma and reincarnation.

** Mystic Qabalah is a spiritual and mystical practice derived from the Jewish Kabbalah but adapted to incorporate Western Hermetic traditions. It involves using symbols and numerology to understand the universe and oneself better.

** Dion Fortune was a British occultist, writer, and teacher who significantly developed the Western Mystery Tradition. She was a mysticism, psychology, and esotericism student, and her teachings and writings influenced many occult practitioners. Her works include "The Mystical Qabalah," "Esoteric Philosophy of Love and Marriage," and "The Sea Priestess."

The Perfect Discourse of Hermes Trismegistus, also known as Asclepius, is a profound and insightful text that delves into the nature of God, the universe, and humanity. This ancient text is believed to have been written by the legendary figure of Hermes Trismegistus, who was known as the "thrice-great" god of wisdom and magic. The discourse begins with Hermes Trismegistus approaching his disciple, Asclepius, who is pondering the nature of God. Hermes then proceeds to unravel the mysteries of the universe and the nature of God through a series of dialogues with his disciple.

According to Hermes, the universe is a living entity, and everything within it is interconnected. The cosmos manifests the divine will, and everything in existence reflects God's infinite wisdom and intelligence. Hermes explains that God is both transcendent and immanent, meaning that he exists beyond the physical universe and within every one of us. God is the source of all life, the universe's creator, and every living being reflected his divine essence.

The Perfect Discourse of Hermes Trismegistus is a text of great wisdom and insight. It is a testament to the ancient world's understanding of the universe and the nature of God, and it continues to inspire and enlighten people to this day.

Life After Death

— OUR JOURNEY CONTINUES... —

Chapter 5

NEAR DEATH EXPERIENCE (NDE)

Definition Of Near-Death Experience (Nde)

A near-death experience (NDE) is a profound personal experience associated with death or impending death that researchers claim shares similar characteristics. When positive, such experiences may encompass a variety of sensations, including detachment from the body, feelings of levitation, total serenity, security, warmth, the experience of absolute dissolution, and the presence of light. Negative experiences may include anguish, distress, a void, devastation, and vast emptiness. People often report seeing hellish places and things like their rendition of "the devil." (Bush and Greyson, 1a) (Sleuties *et al.*, 2a) (French, 3a)

102

Near-death experiences (NDEs) have been the subject of scholarly investigation for many years, and there is no uniformly accepted definition of this phenomenon (Bush and Greyson, 1a). Generally, an NDE is described as an experience when a person is close to death and involves encounters with people they knew during their earthly life (Bush and Greyson, 1a). This kind of experience usually involves an out-of-body experience, which is the apparent separation of consciousness from the body (Bush and Greyson, 1a). NDEs occur when the individual is physically compromised, such as unconscious, comatose, or clinically dead (Bush and Greyson, 1a). During a life review, the individual may gain insight into what others were feeling and thinking during their interactions (Bush and Greyson, 1a). To be classified as an NDE, there must be a score of seven or above on the NDE Scale, and the experience must be reasonably lucid and not fragmentary or brief (Bush and Greyson, 1a). Furthermore, NDErs are generally unconscious or clinically dead during their experiences and should not have any rational or organized memories from their time of unconsciousness (Bush and Greyson, 1a). NDEs are believed to be medically inexplicable and cannot be explained by known physical brain function [1].

Features Of Near-Death Experience

NDEs have been described in the literature as a spectrum of experiences including, but not limited to, life review, mystical union, a sense of having an out-of-body experience, being surrounded by light and entities, traveling through a tunnel, and an awareness that death is not the end (Bush and Greyson, 1a). Despite being widely described, these events remain medically inexplicable (Bush and Greyson, 1a). As such, the nine lines of evidence converge on the conclusion that NDEs are real phenomena, but the cause remains unknown. NDEs can be triggered by various life-threatening events such as a heart attack, cardiac arrest, stroke, near-drowning, coma, drug overdose, or any other situation in which the person fears they may die. Sometimes, people report having a near-death experience even when not in a life-threatening condition. The most common features of NDEs include a sense of peace and well-being, a feeling of being outside of the body, a mind of traveling through a tunnel or dark void, the presence of light, the emotion of being in another realm, and the feeling of being surrounded by benevolent entities. The experience of time distortion is also common, with some people reporting that their entire experience seemed to occur in a matter of seconds, even though it may have lasted for hours.

How People Describe Nde

The research conducted in the Netherlands provides insight into the phenomenon of near-death experiences (Sleuties et al., 2a). As evidenced by the 344 patients successfully resuscitated after cardiac arrest in ten Dutch hospitals (Blanke, 4a), these events can occur in various contexts and with different intensity levels. People who report an NDE after a life-threatening crisis are affected by the frequency, depth, and content of the experience (Blanke, 4a), and the routes by which they attribute meaning to the incident are often similar. Common features of NDEs include hearing a voice, seeing the light, and having a sense of peace and love (Sleuties et al., 2a). Furthermore, the depth of an experience is affected by sex, surviving CPR outside the hospital, and fear before cardiac arrest (Blanke, 4a). The occurrence of an NDE is not associated with the duration of cardiac arrest or unconsciousness, and more patients who had an NDE, especially a deep experience, died within 30 days of cardiac arrest (Blanke, 4a). The study focused on the memories of people who had experienced cardiac arrest (Sleuties et al., 2a). Participants of the research described the NDE as "peaceful," "spiritual," and "surreal." They also reported feeling as though they were in a different realm, disconnected from their physical bodies.

Furthermore, some participants described a sense of pure joy and an intense feeling of love and acceptance. On the other hand, some people experience feelings of anxiety and fear. In some cases, participants experienced a sensation of being pulled or a sense of being separated from their physical bodies. Interestingly, some participants also reported visions of deceased family members or religious figures. The research also revealed that most participants experienced some form of derealization, a feeling of detachment from reality. In addition, many participants did not want to return to their physical bodies. Overall, the research provides insight into how people describe their near-death experiences.

Common Experiences Reported (Ndes)

Near-death experiences (NDEs) are powerful phenomena that profoundly affect a person's life.]. While the cause of an NDE is still unknown (Blanke, 4a), research indicates that the experience can lead to profound changes in attitudes and behaviors that can lead to psychosocial and psychospiritual problems (Bush and Greyson, 1a). Moreover, resistance to a terrifying NDE is likely to intensify fearfulness in an individual, and a similar effect occurs within society when a frightening NDE is resisted and misunderstood (French, 3a). Ultimately, NDEs are powerful experiences that can impact the individual's life (Blanke, 4a).

People from various backgrounds have reported near-death experiences (NDEs) [6]. Research into the phenomenon has become more rigorous in recent years as researchers have sought to understand better the mechanisms and effects of NDEs [5]. NDEs are typically characterized by intense and  generally positive emotions, a life review, a perception of seeing and hearing apart from the physical body, a mystical light, a passage through a tunnel, and a choice to return to their earthly life [6]. NDErs often report encountering deceased loved ones and observing temporal events far from their bodies and beyond possible physical and sensory awareness [6]. NDERF has received scores of NDEs with such observations, later confirmed as factual [6]. NDErs also commonly report feelings of unity with the universe and those who have died [7] and intense positive emotions [6]. To measure the manifestations of NDEs, researchers developed a 33-item scaled-response preliminary questionnaire, which was later reduced to a 16-item NDE scale with high internal consistency, split-half reliability, and test-retest reliability [5]. This scale is also highly correlated with Ring's Weighted Core Experience Index [5]. Although no universally accepted definition of

NDE exists, the phenomenon is generally defined as having both a near-death and experience component [6]. People have reported consistent near-death experiences since antiquity [5], and over 500 people worldwide have experienced an NDE [6]. Interestingly, NDEs from different cultures share similar content [6], with the universal pattern involving feelings of peace, being 'surrounded' with loved ones, and seeing a bright light [7].

How Nde Differs From Other Spiritual Experiences

Near-death experiences (NDEs) are a unique type of spiritual experience that differs from other spiritual experiences in several ways. Unlike different spiritual experiences, NDEs are triggered by life-threatening situations. They are more loosely defined, referring to subjective phenomena, often including an out-of-body experience (OBE) [8]. Research has found that people with NDEs are more likely to believe in a spiritual afterlife [7]. NDEs correlate with greater posttraumatic growth than close brushes with death without such an experience [9], suggesting that NDEs can have a lasting positive impact on those who experience them, perhaps due to the neurological framework established for studying NDEs [8].

The Science Of Near-Death Experiences

Research into near-death experiences (NDEs) has recently increased [3]. The Departments of Behavioral Medicine and Psychiatry at the

University of Virginia Medical Center and the Department of Psychiatry at the University of Michigan Medical Center have studied NDEs [4]. In one such study, 96 individuals who self-reported NDEs and 38 individuals who had come close to death but not had NDEs were given a questionnaire that measured the depth of the experience and dissociative symptoms [5]. Mann-Whitney U tests were used to compare median scores between the two groups [5]. Spearman's rank-order correlation was used to test the association between the depth of NDE and dissociative symptoms [5]. Results indicated that people who reported NDEs experienced significantly more dissociative symptoms than the comparison group [5]. The level of dissociative symptoms among those who said NDEs was also substantially lower than that of patients with pathological dissociative disorders [5].

Furthermore, the depth of the NDE was positively correlated with the level of dissociative symptoms experienced by the NDE group [5]. This pattern of results  suggests that NDEs are linked to dissociation and that the experience is consistent with a non-pathological dissociative response to stress, not a psychiatric disorder [5]. It is also believed that a greater understanding of the dissociation mechanism may help shed further light on NDEs and other mystical or transcendental experiences [5]. NDEs also pose challenges to materialist reductionist models of consciousness, and so further empirical investigation of NDEs presents an opportunity for the discipline of psychology to contribute to ongoing debates about the nature of consciousness [3]. The studies evaluated in the paper discussed included data on 123 cases of in-hospital and out-of-hospital cardiac arrest, with sample sizes varying from 1 to 112 [6]. It was found that near-death experiences (NDEs) were reported by 23% of the interviewed patients who had survived a cardiac arrest,13% of the interviewed patients who reported an NDE during a prior life-threatening illness [7], and 4% of surveyed participants [8].

Additionally, the transcendent state was reported to be a state of relaxed wakefulness in a phenomenologically different space-time. It was consistently associated with slowed breathing, respiratory suspension, reduced muscle activity, and EEG alpha blocking with external stimuli [9]. Moreover, NDEs were significantly associated with younger age, and there was no influence of unconsciousness, duration of arrest, or medication on the experiences [9], while sedation was reported in 40% of cases [6]. Furthermore, the total patient recall was reported in 40% of cases, and most issues involved manually provided compressions [6]. The quality of the studies was evaluated using the Quality Assessment Tool [9], and the median EQ-5D-5L index value among IHCA survivors was 0.78 [6], significantly lower than the general population. The median EQ VAS value among IHCA survivors was 70 [6]. The study's findings confirmed and extended the findings of three smaller studies published within the past year. A new 20-item scale was developed based on the results and most recent empirical evidence, which had very good psychometric properties, including good internal consistency and concurrent validity. It should facilitate future research on near-death experiences [9].

CHART 5.1 SHOWS THE CONFLATION OF RESEARCHERS INTO NDE

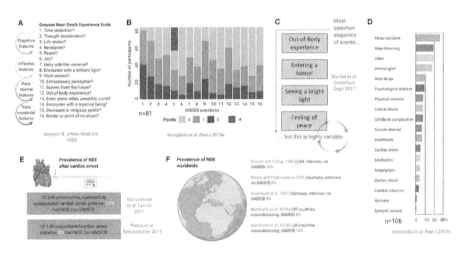

Sources : Greyson et al. 1983; Kondziella et al. Peer Journal 2019a, 2019b; Martial et al. Conscious Cognition 2017: Van Lommel et al. Lancet 2011; Parnia et al. Resuscitation 2014; Proctor and Gallup, 1982; Perea and Padmasekara 2005; Knoblauch et al. 2001.

Unlocking The Mysteries Of Nde: Recent Discoveries And Key Findings

Numerous studies have been conducted to understand better near-death experiences (NDEs) and the associated out-of-body experiences (OBEs). [1]. *Near-Death-Experience Research Forum (NDERF)* surveyed 1122 NDErs asking how they currently view the reality of their experience [1]. The study reviewed 617 NDEs that were sequentially shared on the NDERF website and found that 287 NDEs had OBEs with sufficient information to allow objective determination of the reality of their descriptions of their observations during the OBEs [1]. After reviewing these 287 OBEs, 97.6% of the OBE descriptions were entirely realistic and lacked any content that seemed unreal [1]. Furthermore, 23% of the NDErs with OBEs personally investigated the accuracy of their OBE observations after recovering from their life-threatening event. None of them found any

110

inaccuracy in their OBE observations [1]. In addition, Dr. Janice Holden reviewed NDEs with OBEs in all previously published scholarly articles and books and found 89 case reports [1]. Two large retrospective studies investigated the accuracy of out-of-body observations during near-death experiences [1]. Dr. Michael Sabom conducted the first study and the second by NDERF [1]. Both groups were asked to describe their resuscitation, and the NDE group was found to be much more accurate in their descriptions [1]. The control group without NDEs could have been more accurate and often could only guess what occurred during their resuscitations [1]. Furthermore, a study by NDERF found that 92% of the case reports were completely accurate with no inaccuracy whatsoever when the OBE observations were later investigated [1]. These findings can be used to better understand near-death experiences by providing insight into people's experiences during these events, including the out-of-body knowledge and the ability to describe events that occur [1] accurately. Additionally, these near-death experiences may involve heightened consciousness or awareness during medical emergencies and may not be explained by known physical brain function [1]. Near-death experiences that describe accurate observations while the person was clinically comatose provide further evidence. The high percentage of real out-of-body comments during near-death occasions cannot be explained by any physical brain function known currently [1]. These findings could be used to better understand the phenomenon of near-death experiences and explore the possibility of consciousness beyond physical death [1].

In the US, an estimated 9 million people have reported an NDE, according to a 2011 study in the Annals of the New York Academy of Sciences. Most of these near-death experiences result from a serious injury that affects the body or brain.[9]

111

French psychologist and epistemologist Victor Egger proposed the equivalent French term 'expérience de mort imminente' ("experience of imminent death") to reduce tension in the 1890s among philosophers and psychologists concerning climbers' stories of the panoramic life review during falls.[12][13] In 1892 a series of subjective observations by workers falling from scaffolds, war soldiers who suffered injuries, climbers who had fallen from heights, or other individuals who had come close to death (near drownings, accidents) was reported by Albert Heim being the first time the phenomenon was described as a clinical syndrome.[14] In 1968 Celia Green published an analysis of 400 first-hand accounts of out-of-body experiences [15], representing the first attempt to provide a taxonomy of such experiences, viewed simply as anomalous perceptual experiences or hallucinations. In 1969, Swiss-American psychiatrist and pioneer in near-death studies Elisabeth Kübler-Ross published her book On Death and Dying: What the Dying Have to Teach Doctors, Nurses, Clergy, and Their Own Families. These experiences were also popularized by the work of psychiatrist Raymond Moody, who in 1975 coined the term "near-death experience" as an umbrella term for the different elements (out-of-body experiences, the "panoramic life review," the light, the tunnel, or the border).[14] The term "near-death experience" had already been used by John C. Lilly in 1972.[16]

Common Elements Of Nde

Researchers have identified the common elements that define near-death experiences.[6] Bruce Greyson argues that the general features of the experience include impressions of being outside one's physical body, visions of deceased relatives and religious figures, and the transcendence of 'egotic' and spatiotemporal boundaries.[17] Many common elements have been reported, although the person's interpretation of these events often corresponds with the cultural, philosophical, or religious beliefs of the person experiencing it. For example, in the US, where 46% of the population believes in guardian angels, they will often be identified as angels or deceased loved ones (or will be unidentified). In contrast, Hindus often identify them as messengers of the God of death.[18][19]

Common traits that have been reported by NDErs are as follows:

- A sense/awareness of being dead.[6]
- A sense of peace, well-being, and painlessness. Positive emotions. A sense of removal from the world.[6]
- An out-of-body experience. A perception of one's body from the outside, sometimes observing medical professionals performing resuscitation.[6][20]
- A "tunnel experience" or entering darkness. A sense of moving up or through a passageway or staircase.[6][20]
- A rapid movement toward and sudden immersion in a powerful light (or "Being of Light") communicates telepathically with the person.[21]
- An intense feeling of unconditional love and acceptance.[22]
- Encountering "Beings of Light," "Beings dressed in white," or similar. Also, the possibility of being reunited with deceased loved ones.[6][20]
- Experiencing euphoric environments.[23]
- Receiving a life review, commonly called "seeing one's life flash before one's eyes."[6]
- Approaching a border or a decision by oneself or others to return to one's body is often accompanied by a reluctance to return.[6][20]
- Suddenly finding oneself back inside one's body.[24]
- Connection to the individual's cultural beliefs dictates some of the phenomena experienced in the NDE but more so affects the later interpretation.
- Meeting the dead and hallucinating ghosts in an afterlife environment.[23]

It is also important not to confuse an out-of-body experience (OBE) with a near-death experience. An OBE is part of an NDE, but most importantly, it can happen in other instances than when a person is about to die, such as fainting, deep sleep, and alcohol or drug use [25] where there are many cases of people claiming to have lived through an OBE, seeing the world outside of their physical body.

STAGES NDE

A 1975 study by psychiatrist Raymond Moody, MD, Ph.D., on around 150 patients who claimed to have witnessed an NDE stated that such an experience has nine steps.

The exact description of these nine steps, through Dr. Moody's study, are: [25]

- Sudden peace and relief from pain.
- Perception of a relaxing sound or other-worldly music.
- Consciousness or spirit ascending above the person's body and remotely viewing the attempts at resuscitation from the ceiling (autoscopy).
- The person's soul leaves the earthly realm and climbs rapidly through a tunnel of light in a universe of darkness.
- Arriving at a brilliant "heavenly place."
- They were being met by "people of the light," usually deceased friends and family, in a joyous reunion.
- Meeting with a deity is often perceived as their religious culture would have perceived them or as an intense mass emitting pure love and light.
- In the presence of the Creator, the person undergoes a quick life review and understands how all the good and bad they have done has affected them and others.
- The person returns to their earthly body and life because either they are told it is not their time to die, or they are given a choice and return for the benefit of their family and loved ones.

Moody also explained how not every NDE will have each of these steps and how it could differ for every experience. Due to the potential confusion or shock attributed to those who experience near-death adventures, it is important to treat them calmly and understand right after returning from the Afterlife.

Dr. Moody describes the correct approach to an NDE patient as to "Ask, Listen, Validate, Educate, and Refer"[25]

Kenneth Ring (1980) subdivided the NDE into a five-stage continuum, using Moody's nine-step experiment as inspiration. The subdivisions were: [26]

- Peace
- Body Separation
- Entering darkness
- Seeing the light
- Entering another realm of existence through the light
- Entering night, seeing the light
- There is also a final stage in NDEs: the person in question returning to their life on Earth.[27]

Charlotte Martial, a neuropsychologist from the University of Liège and the University Hospital of Liège who led a team that investigated 154 NDE cases, concluded that there is no fixed sequence of events.[28] Yvonne Kason, MD, classified near-death experiences into three types: the "Out-of-Body" type, the "Mystical" or "White-Light" type, and the "Distressing" type.[29]

CLINICAL CIRCUMSTANCES OF NDE

Kenneth Ring argues that NDEs experienced following attempted suicides are statistically no more unpleasant than NDEs resulting from other situations. [30]

In one series of NDEs, 22% occurred during general anesthesia. [31]

In his study, Bruce Greyson declares that NDEs lack precision in diagnosis. Hence, Dr. Greyson ventured into the study of common effects, mechanisms, sensations, and reactions revealed through NDE survivors by creating a questionnaire of 80 characteristics linked to NDE. He performed many studies averaging 70 responders per study. Nevertheless, he believed that his preliminary form wasn't precise enough, so Dr. Greyson went on to extend his research through tests and analysis, collecting essential data that resulted in him coming up with an exemplary scale for many researchers to use for their studies (See Chart 5.1) [32].

According to the Rasch rating scale, these sixteen multiple-choice questionnaires can be universally applied to all NDEs. It yields the same results no matter the age and gender of the victim, the intensity of the experience, or how much time elapsed between taking the survey and the NDE itself. With the results ranging from 0 to 32, the average score is 15, and the one standard deviation below the mean is 7. Scores below 7 are a subtle NDE, while 8 is considered a "deep" one. An NDE recorded above 8 is stated to be intense. [33]

CHART 10.2   Bruce Greyson's Composition of Final (16-point) NDE
Scale[32]

Component and Question	Weighted Response
Did time seem to speed up?	2 = Everything seemed to be happening all at once
	1 = Time seemed to go faster than usual
	0 = Neither
Were your thoughts speeded up?	2 = Incredibly fast
	1 = Faster than usual
	0= Neither
Did scenes from your past come back to you?	2 = Past flashed before me, out of my control
	1 = Remembered many past events
	0 = Neither
Did you suddenly seem to understand everything?	2 = About the universe
	1 = About myself or others
	0 = Neither
Did you have a feeling of peace or pleasantness?	2 = Incredible peace or pleasantness
	1 = Relief or calmness
	0 = Neither
Did you have a feeling of joy?	2 = Incredible joy
	1 = Happiness
	0 = Neither
Did you feel a sense of harmony or unity with the universe?	2 = United, one with the world
	1 = No longer in conflict with nature
	0 = Neither
Did you see or feel surrounded by a brilliant light?	2 = Light clearly of mystical or other-worldly origin
	1 = Unusually bright light

	0 = Neither
Were your senses more vivid than usual?	2 = Incredibly more so
	1 = More so than usual
	0 = Neither
Did you seem to be of things going on elsewhere, as if by ESP?	2 = Yes, and facts later corroborated
	1 = Yes, but facts not yet corroborated
	0 = Neither
Did scenes from the future come to you?	2 = From the world's future
	1 = From personal future
	0 = Neither
Did you feel separated from your physical body?	2 = left the body and existed outside it
	1 = Lost awareness of the body
	0 = Neither
Did you seem to enter some other, unearthly world?	2 = mystical or unearthly realm
	1 = Unfamiliar, strange place
	0 = Neither
Did you seem to encounter a mystical being or presence?	2 = Definite being or voice clearly of mystical or other-worldly origin
	1 = Unidentifiable voice
	0 = Neither
Did you see deceased spirits or religious figures?	2 = Saw them
	1 = Sensed their presence
	0 = Neither
Did you come to a border or point of no return?	2 = A barrier I was not permitted to cross; or "sent back" to life involuntarily
	1 = A conscious decision to "return" to life
	0 = Neither

Sources:

Journal of Near-Death Studies, 8 (3) Spring © Human Science Press 1990. It is reproduced with kind permission. Source: Near-Death Encounters With and Without Near-Death Experiences: Comparative NDE Scale Profiles, Bruce Greyson, M.D. The University of Connecticut. Also, the following is the Abstract by Professor Bruce Greyson, M.D., from the above-cited journal and included in this book with the kind permission of Professor Bruce Grayson, M.D.

In a retrospective study contrasting the near-death encounters of 183 persons who reported near-death experiences and 63 persons who reported said-death incidents, the two groups did not differ in age, gender, or time elapsed since the near-death encounter. Near-death 'experiencers' report all 16 items of the NDE Scale significantly more often than non-experiencers.

The Greyson scale has helped many researchers advance and enrich their discoveries, especially Dr. Long. Jeffrey Long set out to discover the 'reality' of near-death experiences mostly linked to cardiac arrest victims by using this scale and reviewing NDERF studies.[34] His first line of evidence shows that 835 out of 1122 NDE victims seemed to feel an increase in alertness and consciousness, while studies proved no sign of electrical brain activity. His second line of evidence studies the rise of accuracy developed by NDE survivors defining their resuscitation process with a 97.6% accuracy rate. Dr. Long goes even further in his research with 7 more lines of evidence pointing to realism in NDE experiences. Yet, they are not verifiable or defined by today's medical advances and technology. Having such an abnormally large amount (95.6% out of 1000 participants) of NDE victims proclaiming NDEs as real experiences, it is reasonable to assume that they might be inexplicably real. In short, a doctor's research combined with 35 years of research has only promoted NDE as medically inexplicable,

119

yet most probably a real phenomenon. [35]. Professor Greyson requested this author to point out that many genuine NDE experiencers could not be included in formal studies due to not meeting the high selection criterion for inclusion. Professor Greyson acknowledges these cases were not lacking credibility, and the subjects themselves often reported triggers of life-changing events resulting from their NDE.

The After-Effects Of Near-Death Experience (Nde)

NDEs are associated with changes in personality and outlook on life. [6] Dr. Kenneth Ring [26] has identified consistent values and belief changes related to people with near-death experiences. With these changes, he found a greater appreciation for life, higher self-esteem, greater compassion for others, less concern for acquiring material wealth, a heightened sense of purpose and self-understanding, a desire to learn, elevated spirituality, greater ecological sensitivity and planetary crisis, a feeling of being more intuitive,[6] no longer worrying about death, and claiming to have witnessed an afterlife.[36] While people who have experienced NDEs become more spiritual, it doesn't mean they become necessarily more religious.[37] However, not all after-effects are beneficial[38], and Greyson describes circumstances where changes in attitudes and behavior can lead to psychosocial and psychospiritual problems.[39]

Historical Reports Of Near-Death Experiences

NDEs have been recorded since ancient times.[40] The oldest known medical report of near-death experiences was written by Pierre-Jean du Monchaux, an 18th-century French military doctor who described such a case in his book "Anecdotes de Médecine."[41] Monchaux hypothesized that an influx of blood in the brain stimulated a strong feeling in the individual and therefore caused a near-death experience.[41] In the 19th century, a few

120

studies moved beyond individual cases - one was privately done by members of the Church of Jesus Christ of Latter-day Saints[42] and one in Switzerland. Up to 2005, 95% of world cultures are known to have made some mention of NDEs.[40]

Several more contemporary sources report the incidence of near-death experiences as:

o   17% amongst critically ill patients in nine prospective studies from four countries.[43]

o   10-20% of people have come close to death.[14]

Near-Death Experience Studies

As already mentioned, Bruce Greyson (psychiatrist), Kenneth Ring (psychologist), and Michael Sabom (cardiologist) helped to launch the field of near-death studies and introduced the analysis of near-death experiences to the academic setting. From 1975 to 2005, some 2,500 self-reported individuals in the US were reviewed in retrospective studies of the phenomena[40], with an additional 600 outside the US in the West [40] and 70 in Asia.[40] Additionally, prospective studies identified 270 individuals. Future studies review groups of individuals (e.g., selected emergency room patients) and then find who had an NDE during the study's time; such studies cost more.[40] In all, close to 3,500 individual cases between 1975 and 2005 were reviewed in one or another study. All these studies were carried out by some 55 researchers or teams of researchers.[40]

Melvin L. Morse, head of the Institute for the Scientific Study of Consciousness, and colleagues [20][44] have investigated near-death experiences in a pediatric population.[45]

Clinical Research In Cardiac Arrest Patients Parnia's Study

121

In 2001, Sam Parnia and colleagues published the results of a year-long study of cardiac arrest survivors conducted at Southampton General Hospital. Sixty-three survivors were interviewed. They were resuscitated after being clinically dead with no pulse, respiration, and fixed dilated pupils. Parnia and colleagues investigated out-of-body experience claims by placing figures in areas where patients were likely to be resuscitated on suspended boards facing the ceiling, not visible from the floor. Four had experiences that, according to the study criteria, were NDEs, but none experienced the out-of-body experience. Thus, they were not able to identify the figures.[46][47][48]

Psychologist Chris French wrote regarding the study, "Unfortunately, and somewhat atypically, none of the survivors in this sample experienced an out-of-body experience."[47]

Pim Van Lommel's Study

In 2001, Pim van Lommel, a cardiologist from the Netherlands, and his team conducted a study on NDEs, including 344 cardiac arrest patients who had been successfully resuscitated in 10 Dutch hospitals. Patients not reporting NDEs were used as controls for patients who did, and psychological (e.g., fear before cardiac arrest), demographic (e.g., age, sex), medical (e.g., more than one cardiopulmonary resuscitation (CPR)), and pharmacological data were compared between the two groups. The work also included a longitudinal study where the two groups (those with an NDE and those without one) were compared at two and eight years for life changes. One patient had a conventional out-of-body experience. He reported being able to watch and recall events during his cardiac arrest. His claims were confirmed by hospital personnel. "This did not appear consistent with hallucinatory or illusory experiences, as the recollections were compatible with real and verifiable rather than imagined events."[48][49]

Awareness During Resuscitation (Aware) Study

While at the University of Southampton, Parnia was the principal investigator of the AWARE study, which was launched in 2008.[13] This study which concluded in 2012, included 33 investigators across 15 medical centers in the UK, Austria, and the US and tested consciousness, memories, and awareness during cardiac arrest. The accuracy of visual and auditory awareness claims was examined using specific tests.[50] One such test consisted of installing shelves bearing various images and facing the ceiling, hence not visible to hospital staff, in rooms where cardiac-arrest patients were more likely to occur. The study results were published in October 2014; both the launch and the study results were widely discussed in the media.[51][52]

A review article analyzing the results reports that out of 2,060 cardiac arrest events, 101 of 140 cardiac arrest survivors could complete the questionnaires. Of these 101 patients, 9% could be classified as near-death experiences. Two more patients (2% of those completing the questionnaires) described "seeing and hearing actual events related to the period of cardiac arrest." These two patients' cardiac arrests did not occur in areas with ceiling shelves; hence, no images could be used to test visual awareness claims objectively. One of the two patients was too sick, and the accuracy of her recount could not be verified. For the second patient, however, it was possible to verify the accuracy of the experience and to show that awareness occurred paradoxically some minutes after the heart stopped at a time when "the brain ordinarily stops functioning, and cortical activity becomes isoelectric (i.e., without any discernible electric activity)." The experience was incompatible with an illusion, imaginary event, or hallucination since visual (other than ceiling shelves' images) and auditory awareness could be corroborated.[48]

Aware Ii

As of May 2016, a posting at the UK Clinical Trials Gateway website described plans for AWARE II, a two-year multicenter observational study of 900-1500 patients experiencing cardiac arrest, which said that subject recruitment had started on 1 August 2014 and that the scheduled end date was 31 May 2017.[53] The study was extended, continuing until 2020.[54] In 2019, a report of a condensed study with 465 patients was released. Only one patient remembered the auditory stimuli, while none remembered the visual.[53][failed verification]

Meditation-Induced Near-Death Experiences

A three-year longitudinal study has revealed that some Buddhist meditation practitioners can willfully induce near-death experiences at a pre-planned time. Unlike traditional NDEs, participants were conscious of experiencing the meditation-induced NDE and retained control over its content and duration.[55] The Dalai Lama has also asserted that experienced meditators can deliberately cause the NDE state during meditation, being able to recognize and sustain it.[56]

In a review article, psychologist Chris French [47] has grouped approaches to explain NDEs into three broad groups which "are not distinct and independent, but instead show considerable overlap": spiritual theories (also called transcendental), psychological theories, and physiological theories that provide a physical explanation for NDEs.

Spiritual Or Transcendental Theories Of Near-Death Experience

French summarizes this model by saying: "The most popular interpretation is that the NDE is what it appears to be to the person having the experience."[47] The NDE would then represent evidence of the supposedly immaterial existence of a soul or mind, which would leave the body upon death. An NDE would then provide information about a supernatural world where the soul would journey upon ending its existence on Earth.[47]

According to Greyson[14], some NDE phenomena cannot be easily explained with our current knowledge of human physiology and psychology. For instance, when they were unconscious, patients could accurately describe events and report being able to view their bodies "from an out-of-body spatial perspective." In two studies of patients who had survived a cardiac arrest, those who had reported leaving their bodies could accurately describe their resuscitation procedures or unexpected events, whereas others "described incorrect equipment and procedures."[14] Sam Parnia also refers to two cardiac arrest studies and one deep hypothermic circulatory arrest study where patients reported visual and auditory awareness occurring when their brain function had ceased. These reports "were corroborated with actual and real events."[57][48]

Five prospective studies have been carried out to test the accuracy of out-of-body perceptions by placing "unusual targets in locations likely to be seen by persons having NDEs, such as in an upper corner of a room in the emergency department, the coronary care unit, or the intensive care unit of a hospital." Twelve patients reported leaving their bodies, but none could describe the hidden visual targets. Although this is a small sample, the failure of purported out-of-body 'experiencers' to explain the remote targets raises questions about the accuracy of the anecdotal reports described above.[14]

Some patients floated in the opposite direction of the targets.

Some patients were floating just above the body, thus not high enough to see the targets.

One patient reported being too focused on observing the body to look for marks. Also, he alleges that he could see them if he had told him to look for them.

Psychologist James Alcock has described the afterlife claims of NDE researchers as pseudoscientific. Alcock has written that the spiritual or transcendental interpretation "is based on belief in search of data rather than observation in search of an explanation."[58] Chris French has noted that "the survivalist approach does not appear to generate clear and testable hypotheses. Because of the vagueness and imprecision of the survivalist account, it can be made to explain any possible set of findings and is therefore unfalsifiable and unscientific."[59]

Physiological Explanations Of Near-Death Experiences

A wide range of physiological theories of the NDE has been put forward, including those based upon cerebral hypoxia, anoxia, and hypercapnia; endorphins and other neurotransmitters; and abnormal activity in the temporal lobes. [47]

Researchers in medical science and psychiatry have investigated neurobiological factors in the experience. [64] Among the researchers and commentators who tend to emphasize a naturalistic and neurological base for the background is the British psychologist Susan Blackmore (1993), with her "dying brain hypothesis."[65],

French (2014) summarizes the main psychological explanations, including depersonalization, expectancy, and dissociation models. And another model [47]

Depersonalization Model

A depersonalization model was proposed in the 1970s by professor of psychiatry Russell Noyes and clinical psychologist Roy Kletti, which suggested that the NDE is a form of depersonalization experienced under emotional conditions such as life-threatening danger, potentially inescapable danger, and that the NDE can best be understood as a hallucination.[47][60][61][62][63] According to this model, those who face impending death become detached from their surroundings and bodies, no longer feel emotions and experience time distortions.[14]

This model suffers from several limitations in explaining NDEs for subjects who do not experience a sensation of being out of their bodies; unlike NDEs, experiences are dreamlike, unpleasant, and characterized by "anxiety, panic, and emptiness."[14] Also, during NDEs, subjects remain very lucid of their identities, and their sense of identity is not changed, unlike those experiencing depersonalization. [14]

Expectancy Model

Another psychological theory is called the expectancy model. It has been suggested that although these experiences could appear very real, they had been constructed in mind, either consciously or subconsciously, in response to the stress of an encounter with death (or perceived encounter with death) and did not correspond to a real event. In a way, they are like wish-fulfillment: because someone thought they were about to die, experiencing certain things following what they expected or wanted to occur.

127

Imagining a heavenly place was, in effect, a way for them to soothe themselves through the stress of knowing they were close to death.[47] Subjects use their personal and cultural expectations to imagine a scenario protecting them against an imminent threat to their lives.[14]

Subjects' accounts often differed from their "religious and personal expectations regarding death," which contradicts the hypothesis that they may have imagined a scenario based on their cultural and personal background. [14]

Although the term NDE was first coined in 1975 and the experience first described then, recent descriptions of NDEs are like those reported earlier than 1975. The only exception is the more frequent description of a tunnel. Hence, the fact that information about these experiences could be more easily obtained after 1975 did not influence people's reports of the incidents. [14]

Another flaw of this model can be found in children's accounts of NDEs. These are similar to adults, despite children being less strongly affected by religious and cultural influences about death. [14]

Dissociation Model

The dissociation model proposes that NDE is a form of withdrawal to protect an individual from a stressful event. Under extreme circumstances, some people may detach from certain unwanted feelings to avoid experiencing the emotional impact and suffering associated with them. The person also separates from one's immediate surroundings. [47]

Birth Model

The birth model suggests that near-death experiences could be a form of reliving the birth trauma. Since a baby's journey from the womb's darkness is greeted by the love and warmth of the nursing and medical staff, it was proposed that the dying brain could be recreating the passage through a tunnel to light, heat, and affection. [47]

Reports of leaving the body through a tunnel are equally frequent among subjects born by cesarean section and natural birth. Also, newborns do not possess "the visual acuity, spatial stability of their visual images, mental alertness, and cortical coding capacity to register memories of the birth experience."[14]

Neuroanatomical Models

Neuroscientists Olaf Blanke and Sebastian Dieguez (2009),[66] from the Ecole Polytechnique Fédérale de Lausanne, Switzerland, propose a brain-based model with two types of NDEs:

"type 1 NDEs are due to bilateral frontal and occipital, but predominantly right hemispheric brain damage affecting the right temporal-parietal junction and characterized by out-of-body experiences, altered sense of time, sensations of flying, lightness 'vection' and flying"[4]

"type 2 NDEs are also due to bilateral frontal and occipital, but predominantly left hemispheric brain damage affecting the left temporal, parietal junction and characterized by a feeling of a presence, meeting, and communication with spirits, seeing of glowing bodies, as well as voices, sounds, and music without 'vection'"[4]

They suggest that damage to the bilateral occipital cortex may lead to visual features of NDEs, such as seeing a tunnel or lights, and "damage to unilateral or bilateral temporal lobe structures such as the hippocampus and amygdala" may lead to emotional experiences, memory flashbacks or a life review. They concluded that future neuroscientific studies would likely reveal the neuroanatomical basis of the NDE, which will lead to the demystification of the subject without needing paranormal explanations. [4]

Neurochemical Models

Some theories explain they reported NDE experiences as resulting from drugs used during resuscitation (in the case of 'resuscitation induced' NDEs) — for example, ketamine — or from endogenous chemicals that transmit signals between brain cells, neurotransmitters:[47]

In the early eighties, Daniel Carr wrote that the NDE has characteristics that suggest a limbic lobe syndrome and that the NDE can be explained by the release of endorphins and enkephalins in the brain.[68][69] Endorphins are endogenous molecules "released in times of stress and lead to a reduction in pain perception and a pleasant, even blissful, emotional state."[47]

Judson and Wiltshaw (1983) noted how the administration of endorphin-blocking agents such as naloxone had been occasionally reported to produce "hellish" NDEs.[70] would be coherent with endorphins' role in causing a "positive emotional tone of most NDEs."[47]

Morse et al. 1989 proposed a model arguing that serotonin played a more important role than endorphins in generating NDEs [71], "at least concerning mystical hallucinations and OBEs."[47]

A 2019 large-scale study found that ketamine, Salvia divinorum, and DMT (and other classical psychedelic substances) are linked to near-death experiences.[72]

According to Parnia, neurochemical models are not backed by data, which is true for "NMDA receptor activation, serotonin, and endorphin release" models.[48] Parnia writes that no data has been collected via thorough and careful experimentation to back "a possible causal relationship or even an association" between neurochemical agents and NDE experiences.[57]

Multi-Factorial Models

The first formal neurobiological model for NDE included endorphins, neurotransmitters of the limbic system, the temporal lobe, and other brain parts.[73] Extensions and variations of their model came from other scientists, such as Louis Appleby (1989).[74]

Other authors suggest that all components of near-death experiences can be explained via psychological or neurophysiological mechanisms. However, the authors admit that these hypotheses must be tested by science. [75]

Low oxygen levels (and G-LOC) model

Low oxygen levels in the blood (hypoxia or anoxia) have been hypothesized to induce hallucinations and possibly explain NDEs. [18][47] Because low oxygen levels characterize life-threatening situations and the apparent similarities between NDEs and G-force-induced loss of consciousness (G-LOC) episodes.

131

These episodes are observed with fighter pilots experiencing rapid and intense acceleration, resulting in insufficient blood supply to the brain. Whinnery[76] studied almost 1000 cases and noted how the experiences often involved "tunnel vision and bright lights, floating sensations, automatic movement, autoscopy, OBEs, not wanting to be disturbed, paralysis, vivid dreams of beautiful places, pleasurable sensations, psychological alterations of euphoria and dissociation, the inclusion of friends and family, the inclusion of prior memories and thoughts, the experience being very memorable (when it can be remembered), confabulation, and a strong urge to understand the experience."[47][76]

However, acceleration-induced hypoxia's primary characteristics are "rhythmic jerking of the limbs, compromised memory of events just before the onset of unconsciousness, tingling of extremities ..." that are not observed during NDEs.[18] Also, G-LOC episodes do not feature life reviews, mystical experiences, and "long-lasting transformational after-effects." However, this may be because subjects do not expect to die. [47]

Also, hypoxic hallucinations are characterized by "distress and agitation," which is very different from near-death experiences, which subjects report as pleasant. [14]

She Altered Blood Gas Level Models.

Some investigators have studied whether hypercarbia, or higher than normal carbon dioxide levels, could explain the occurrence of NDEs. However, studies are difficult to interpret since NDEs have been observed with increased and decreased carbon dioxide levels. Finally, some other studies observed NDEs when levels had not changed, with little data. [18]

Other Models

According to Engmann (2008), near-death experiences of people who are clinically dead are psychopathological symptoms caused by a severe brain malfunction resulting from the cessation of cerebral blood circulation.[78] An important question is whether it is possible to "translate" the bloomy experiences of the reanimated survivors into 'psychopathologically' basic phenomena, e.g., acoasms (nonverbal auditory hallucinations), central narrowing of the visual field, autoscopia, visual hallucinations, activation of limbic and memory structures according to Moody's stages. The symptoms suppose a primary affliction of the occipital and temporal cortices under clinical death. This basis could be congruent with the thesis of pathoclisis—the inclination of special brain parts to be the first to be damaged in case of disease, lack of oxygen, or malnutrition—established eighty years ago by Cécile Vogt-Mugnier and Oskar Vogt. [79]

Professor of Neurology Terence Hines (2003) claimed that near-death experiences are hallucinations caused by cerebral anoxia, drugs, or brain damage. [80]

Greyson has called into question the adequacy of the materialist mind-brain identity model for explaining NDE.[31] An NDE often involves vivid and complex mentation, sensation, and memory formation under circumstances of complete disabling of brain function during general anesthesia or near-complete cessation of cerebral blood flow and oxygen uptake during cardiac arrest. Materialist models predict that such conscious experiences would be impossible under these conditions. The mind-brain identity model of classic materialist psychology may need to be expanded to explain an NDE adequately.

Cross-Cultural Aspects Of Near-Death Experience (Nde)

Gregory Shushan published an analysis of the afterlife beliefs of five ancient civilizations [81] and compared them with historical and contemporary reports of near-death experiences and shamanic afterlife "journeys." Shushan found similarities across time, place, and culture that he found could not be explained by coincidence; he also found elements that were specific to cultures; Shushan concludes that some form of mutual influence between experiences of an afterlife and culture probably influences one another and that this inheritance, in turn, influences individual NDEs.[82]

In contrast, it has been argued that near-death experiences and many of their elements, such as the vision of God, judgment, the tunnel, or the life review, are closely related to the religious and spiritual traditions of the West. It was mainly Christian visionaries, Spiritualists, Occultists, and Theosophists of the 19th and 20th centuries that reported them.[82] However, according to Parnia, near-death experiences interpretations are influenced by religious, social, and cultural backgrounds. However, the core elements transcend borders and can be considered universal. Children have even reported some of these core elements (this occurred over many months while playing and communicating using children's language). In other words, they are at an age where they should not have been influenced by culture or tradition.[48] Also, according to Greyson [14], the central features of NDEs are universal and have not been affected by time. These have been observed throughout history and in different cultures.

Sources and References – Chapter Five.

1a. Bush NE, Greyson B (November–December 2014). *"Distressing Near-Death Experiences: The Basics." Mo Med. 111 (6): 486–90. PMC 6173534. PMID 25665233.*

2a. Sleutjes, A; Moreira-Almeida, A; Greyson, B (2014). *"Almost 40 years investigating near-death experiences: an overview of mainstream scientific journals". J. Nerv. Ment. Dis. 202 (11): 833–6. doi:10.1097/NMD.0000000000000205. PMID 25357254. S2CID 16765929.*

3a. French Kristen (2022-09-28). *"The Afterlife Is in Our Heads." Nautilus. We retrieved 2022-12-12.*

4a. Blanke, Olaf (2009). *The Neurology of Consciousness. London: London: Academic Publishers, 2009. pp. 303–324. ISBN 978-0-12-374168-4.*

1. Greyson, B., *The Near-Death Experience as a Focus of Clinical Attention. The Journal of Nervous & Mental Disease 185(5): p 327-334, May 1997.*

2. Roberts, G., & Owen, J. (1988*). The Near-death Experience. The British Journal of Psychiatry, 153(5), 607-617. doi:10.1192/bjp.153.5.607*

3. Bush, N.E. *Afterward: Making Meaning After a Frightening Near-Death Experience. Journal of Near-Death Studies 21, 99–133 (2002). https://doi.org/10.1023/A:1021223618666*

4. Knoblauch, H., Schmied, I. & Schnettler, B. *Different Kinds of Near-Death Experience: A Report on a Survey of Near-Death Experiences in Germany. Journal of Near-Death Studies 20, 15–29 (2001). https://doi.org/10.1023/A:1011112727078*

5. Olaf Blanke, Nathan Faivre, & Sebastian Dieguez, *Chapter 20 - Leaving Body and Life Behind: Out-of-Body and Near-Death Experience, The Neurology of Consciousness (Second Edition), Academic Press, 2016, Pages 323-347, ISBN 9780128009482, https://doi.org/10.1016/B978-0-12-800948-2.00020-0.*

6. Griffith, LJ (2009). *"Near-death experiences and psychotherapy." Psychiatry (Edgmont). 6 (10): 35–42. PMC 2790400. PMID 20011577.*

7. Mauro, James. *"Bright lights, the big mystery," Psychology Today, July 1992.*

8. Vanhaudenhuyse, A.; Thonnard, M.; Laureys, S. (2009). *"Towards a Neuro-scientific Explanation of Near-death Experiences?" (PDF). In Vincent, Jean-Louis (ed.). Yearbook of Intensive Care and Emergency Medicine. Berlin, Heidelberg: Springer Berlin Heidelberg. ISBN 978-3-540-92276-6.*

9. Koch, Christof. *"What Near-Death Experiences Reveal about the Brain." Scientific American. They were retrieved on 2020-05-20.*

10. "Can Science Explain Near Death Experiences?" Discover Magazine. They were retrieved on 2022-03-10.

11. Pim van Lommel (2010). *Consciousness Beyond Life: The Science of the near-death experience. HarperOne. ISBN 978-0-06-177725-7.*

12. Evelyn Elsaesser Valarino (1997). *On the Other Side of Life: Exploring the Phenomenon of the near-death experience. Perseus Publishing. p. 203. ISBN 978-0-7382-0625-7.*

13. Egger, Victor (1896). *"Le moi des mourants", Revue Philosophique, XLI: 26-38.*

14. J. Bogousslavsky, M. G. Hennerici, H Bazner, C. Bassetti (Eds.) (2010). *Neurological Disorders in Famous Artists, Part 3. Karger Publishers. p. 189. ISBN 9783805593304.*

15. Greyson, Bruce (2014). *"Chapter 12: Near-Death Experiences". In Cardeña, Etzel; Lynn, Steven Jay; Krippner, Stanley (Eds.). Varieties of anomalous experience: examining the scientific evidence (Second Ed.). Washington, DC: American Psychological Association. pp. 333–367. ISBN 978-1-4338-1529-4.*

16. Green, C., *Out-of-the-body Experiences, London: Hamish Hamilton, 1968.*

17. Schlieter, Jens (2018). *What is it like to be dead? Near-death Experiences, Christianity, and the Occult. New York: Oxford University Press, pp. 205-6.*

18. Greyson, Bruce (2003). *"Near-Death Experiences in a Psychiatric Outpatient Clinic Population." Psychiatric Services. 54 (12): 1649–1651. doi:10.1176/appi.ps.54.12.1649. PMID 14645808.*

19. Holden, Janice Miner; Greyson, Bruce; James, Debbie, eds. (2009). The handbook of near-death experiences is thirty years of investigation. Westport, Conn.: Praeger Publishers. ISBN 978-0-313-35865-4.Kennard, Mary J (1998). "A Visit from an Angel." The American Journal of Nursing. 98 (3): 48–51. doi:10.1097/00000446-199803000-00041. PMID 9536180.

20. Morse, M; Conner, D; Tyler, D (June 1985). "Near-death experiences in a pediatric population. A preliminary report". Am. J. Dis. Child. 139 (6): 595–600. doi:10.1001/archpedi.1985.02140080065034. PMID 4003364.

21. Lovins, LaDonna. "Three Beings of Light." iands.org. They were retrieved on 2018-03-30.

22. Long, Jeffrey (2016-06-29). "Opinion | Stories of God's love common among those who almost die says the doctor who studies them." Washington Post. ISSN 0190-8286. Retrieved 2018-03-27.

23. Newman, Tim (27 April 2016). "Near-death experiences: Fact or fantasy?". MedicalNewsToday.

24. Moody, Raymond (1975). Life After Life. Mockingbird Books. ISBN 978-0-89176-037-5.

25. Hagan III, John C. (November 18, 2018). "The Near-Death Experience: Diagnosis and Treatment Of a Common Medical Syndrome." Clinical Oncology News.

26. Ring, K. (1980). Life at death: A scientific investigation of the near-death experience. New York: Coward, McCann, & Geoghegan., p. 40

27. Hagan III, John C. (November 12, 2018). "The Near-Death Experience: Diagnosis and Treatment Of a Common Medical Syndrome." Clinical Oncology News.

28. "What happens when you die? Scientists attempt to discover how similar near-death experiences are". Newsweek. 2017-07-27. Archived from the original on 2019-12-22 and retrieved 2018-09-26.

29. Kason, Yvonne (2019). Touched by the Light: Exploring Spiritually Transformative Experiences. Toronto, Canada: Dundurn Press. pp. 75–101. ISBN 9781459745513.

30. Ring, Kenneth. Heading toward Omega. In Search of the Meaning of Near-Death Experience, 1984, p. 45. "Subsequent research on suicide-related NDEs by Stephen Franklin and myself [Ring] and by Bruce Greyson has also confirmed my earlier tentative findings the NDEs following suicide attempts, however, induced, conform to the classic prototype."

31. Greyson, Bruce (2010). "Implications of near-death experiences for a postmaterialist psychology." Psychology of Religion and Spirituality. 2 (1): 37–45. doi:10.1037/a0018548.

32. Greyson, Bruce (1983). "The Near-Death Experience Scale Construction, Reliability, and Validity" (PDF). The Journal of Nervous and Mental Disease. 171 (6): 369–375. doi:10.1097/00005053-198306000-00007. PMID 6854303.

33. Khanna, Surbhi; Greyson, Bruce (2014). "Near-Death Experiences and Spiritual Well-Being." Journal of Religion and Health. 53 (6): 1605–1615. doi:10.1007/s10943-013-9723-0. JSTOR 24485267. PMID 23625172. S2CID 8578903. Retrieved 2022-05-12.

34. "Current NDES." Near-Death Experience Research Foundation.

35. Long, Jeffrey (2014). "Near-Death Experiences Evidence for Their Reality." Missouri Medicine. 111 (5): 372–380. PMC 6172100. PMID 25438351.

36. Mendoza, Marilyn A. (12 March 2018). "After-effects of the Near-Death Experience." Psychology Today.

37. Bendix, Aria (19 March 2022). "People describe near-death experiences in an eerily similar way. They've convinced some researchers that an afterlife exists". Business Insider. They were retrieved on 2022-08-15.

38. Orne, RM (June 1995). "The meaning of survival: the early aftermath of a near-death experience." Res Nurs Health. 18 (3): 239–47. doi:10.1002/nur.4770180307. PMID 7754094.

39. Greyson, B (May 1997). "The near-death experience as a focus of clinical attention." J. Nerv. Ment. Dis. 185 (5): 327–34. doi:10.1097/00005053-199705000-00007. PMID 9171810.

40. Holden, Janice Miner; Greyson, Bruce; James, Debbie, eds. (22 June 2009). "The Field of Near-Death Studies: Past, Present, and Future." The Handbook of Near-Death Experiences: Thirty Years of Investigation. Greenwood Publishing Group. pp. 1–16. ISBN 978-0-313-35864-7.

41. Gholipour, Bahar (24 July 2014). "Oldest Medical Report of Near-Death Experience Discovered." Live Science. They were retrieved on 16 October 2018.

42. "The Near-Death Experience | Religious Studies Center." rsc.byu.edu.

43. Zingrone, N L (2009). "Pleasurable Western adult near-death experiences: Features, circumstances, and incidence." In Holden, J M; Greyson, B; James, D (eds.). The Handbook of Near-Death Experiences: Thirty Years of Investigation (2009 ed.). Santa Barbara, California: Praeger-ABC-CLIO. pp. 17–40. ISBN 978-0313358647.

44. Morse M, Castillo P, Venecia D, Milstein J, Tyler DC. (1986) "Childhood near-death experiences." American Journal of Diseases of Children, Nov;140(11):1110–4.

45. Singhji, Sant Rajinder (1 December 2018). "Mystic Mantra: Our soul is immortal." The Deccan Chronicle. Retrieved 17 December 2021.

46. Parnia, S.; Waller, D. G.; Yeates, R.; Fenwick, P. (2001-02-01). "A qualitative and quantitative study of the incidence, features, and etiology of near-death experiences in cardiac arrest survivors." Resuscitation. 48 (2): 149–156. doi:10.1016/s0300-9572(00)00328-2. PMID 11426476.

47. French, Christopher C. (2005-01-01). "Near-death experiences in cardiac arrest survivors." The Boundaries of Consciousness: Neurobiology and Neuropathology. Progress in Brain Research. Vol. 150. pp. 351–367. doi:10.1016/S0079-6123(05)50025-6. ISBN 9780444518514. PMID 16186035.

48. Parnia, Sam (2014-11-01). "Death and consciousness--an overview of the mental and cognitive experience of death." Annals of the New York Academy of Sciences. 1330 (1): 75–93. Bibcode:2014NYASA1330...75P. doi:10.1111/nyas.12582. PMID 25418460. S2CID 33091589.

49. van Lommel, P; van Wees, R; Meyers, V; Elfferich, I (15 December 2001). "Near-death experience in cardiac arrest survivors: a prospective study in the Netherlands." Lancet. 358 (9298): 2039–45. doi:10.1016/S0140-6736(01)07100-8. PMID 11755611. S2CID 29766030.

50. Parnia, Sam; Spearpoint, Ken; de Vos, Gabriele; Fenwick, Peter; Goldberg, Diana; Yang, Jie; Zhu, Jiawen; Baker, Katie; Killingback, Hayley (2014-12-01). "AWARE-Awareness during Resuscitation-a prospective study." Resuscitation. 85 (12): 1799–1805. doi:10.1016/j.resuscitation.2014.09.004. PMID 25301715.

51. Lichfield, Gideon (April 2015). "The science of near-death experiences: Empirically investigating brushes with the afterlife." The Atlantic. The Atlantic. They retrieved 10 October 2016.

52. Weintraub, Pamela (September 2014). "Seeing the light." Psychology Today. Psychology Today. They retrieved 10 October 2016.

53. UK Clinical Trials Gateway. Primary Trial ID Number 17129, entitled "AWARE II (Awareness during Resuscitation) A Multi-Centre Observational Study of the Relationship between the Quality of Brain Resuscitation and Consciousness, Neurological, Functional and Cognitive Outcomes following Cardiac Arrest" Last updated 3 May 2016. Page archived 9 May 2016

54. ^ "AWARE NDE Study | Psi Encyclopedia".

55. ^Van Gordon, William; Shonin, Edo; Dunn, Thomas J.; Sheffield, David; Garcia-Campayo, Javier; Griffiths, Mark D. (2018-12-01). "Meditation-Induced Near-Death Experiences: a 3-Year Longitudinal Study". Mindfulness. 9 (6): 1794–1806. doi:10.1007/s12671-018-0922-3. ISSN 1868-8535. PMC 6244634. PMID 30524512.

56. Bstan-'dzin-rgya-mtsho, Dalai Lama XIV (c. 2006). The universe in a single atom: the convergence of science and spirituality. Broadway Books. ISBN 9780767920810. OCLC 188546206.

57. Parnia, Sam (February 2017). "Understanding the cognitive experience of death and the near-death experience." QJM: An International Journal of Medicine. 110 (2): 67–69. doi:10.1093/qjmed/hcw185. PMID 28100825.

58. Frazier, Kendrick (1981). Paranormal Borderlands of Science. Buffalo, NY: Prometheus Books. pp. 153–169. ISBN 978-0-87975-148-7.

59. French, Chris. (2009). Near-Death Experiences and the Brain. In Craig Murray. Psychological Scientific Perspectives on Out-of-Body and Near-Death Experiences. Nova Science Publishers. pp. 187–203. ISBN 978-1-60741-705-7

60. Noyes, R (1972). "The experience of dying." Psychiatry. 35 (2): 174–184. doi:10.1080/00332747.1972.11023710. PMID 5024906.

61. Noyes, R.; Kletti, R. (1976). "Depersonalisation in the face of life-threatening danger: an interpretation." Omega. 7 (2): 103–114. doi:10.2190/7qet-2vau-ycdt-tj9r. S2CID 144273683.

62. Noyes, R.; Kletti, R. (1977). "Depersonalisation in the face of life-threatening danger." Compr. Psychiatry. 18 (4): 375–384. doi:10.1016/0010-440X(77)90010-4. PMID 872561.

63. Noyes, R. and Slymen, D. (1978-1979) The subjective response to life-threatening danger. Omega 9: 313–321.

64. Mayank and Mukesh, 2004; Jansen, 1995; Thomas, 2004; Fenwick and Fenwick 2008

65. Bassham, Gregory (2005). Critical Thinking: A Student's Introduction (2nd ed.). Boston: McGraw-Hill. p. 485. ISBN 978-0-07-287959-9.

66. Leaving Body And Life Behind:lnco.epfl.ch

67. Vincent, Jean-Louis (2009). "Towards a Neuro-scientific Explanation of Near-death Experiences?". Intensive Care Medicine. [S.l.]: Springer New York. pp. 961–968. CiteSeerX 10.1.1.368.4580. doi:10.1007/978-3-540-92276-6_85. ISBN 978-0-387-92277-5.

68. Carr, Daniel (1981). "Endorphins at the Approach of Death." Lancet. 317 (8216): 390. doi:10.1016/s0140-6736(81)91714-1. S2CID 45806328.

69. Carr, Daniel (1982). "Pathophysiology of Stress-Induced Limbic Lobe Dysfunction: A Hypothesis Relevant to Near-Death Experiences." Anabiosis: The Journal of Near-Death Studies. 2: 75–89.

70. Judson, I. R; Wiltshaw, E. (1983). "A near-death experience." Lancet. 322 (8349): 561–562. doi:10.1016/s0140-6736(83)90582-2. PMID 6136705. S2CID 13016282.

71. Morse, M. L; Venecia, D; Milstein, J. (1989). "Near-death experiences: A neurophysiological explanatory model." Journal of Near-Death Studies. 8: 45–53. doi:10.1007/BF01076138. S2CID 18026980.

72. Martial, C; Cassol, H; Charland-Verville, V; Pallavicini, C; Sanz, C; Zamberlan, F; Vivot, RM; Erowid, F; Erowid, E; Laureys, S; Greyson, B; Tagliazucchi, E (March 2019). "Neurochemical models of near-death experiences: A large-scale study based on the semantic similarity of written reports." Consciousness and Cognition. 69: 52–69. doi:10.1016/j.concog.2019.01.011. hdl:2268/231971. PMID 30711788. S2CID 73432875.

73. Saavedra-Aguilar, J.C.; Gómez-Jeria, Juan S. (1989). "A Neurobiological Model for Near-Death Experiences" (PDF). Journal of Near-Death Studies. 7 (4): 205–222. doi:10.1007/bf01074007. S2CID 189940970. Retrieved 14 August 2020.

74. Appleby, L (1989). "Near-death experience: Analogous to other stress-induced psychological phenomena." British Medical Journal. 298 (6679): 976–977. doi:10.1136/bmj.298.6679.976. PMC 1836313. PMID 2499387.

75. Mobbs, Dean; Watt, Caroline (October 2011). "There is nothing paranormal about near-death experiences: how neuroscience can explain seeing bright lights, meeting the dead, or being convinced you are one of them" (PDF). Trends in Cognitive Sciences. 15 (10): 447–449. doi:10.1016/j.tics.2011.07.010. hdl:20.500.11820/18d7f026-76f4-4d99-8f39-8b6ac51b6069. PMID 21852181. S2CID 6080825.

76. Whinnery, J. E. (1997). "Psychophysiologic correlates of unconsciousness and near-death experiences." J. Near-Death Stud. 15: 231–258.

77. French, Chris (2001). "Dying to Know the Truth: Visions of a Dying Brain, or False Memories?". Lancet. 358 (9298): 2010–2011. doi:10.1016/s0140-6736(01)07133-1. PMID 11755600. S2CID 33004716.

78. Engmann, B (December 2008). "[Near-death experiences: a review of the thesis of pathoclisis, neurotransmitter abnormalities, and psychological aspects]".

MMW Fortschr Med. 150 (51–52): 42–3. doi:10.1007/BF03365763. PMID 19156957. S2CID 79259801.

79. Vogt C, Vogt O. (1922). Erkrankungen der Großhirnrinde im Lichte der Topistik, Pathoklise und Pathoarchitektonik. Journal für Psychologie und Neurologie; Bd. 28. Joh.- Ambr.- Barth- Verlag. Leipzig. (German).

80. Hines, Terence (2002). Pseudoscience and the Paranormal (2nd ed.). Amherst, NY: Prometheus Books. pp. 101–104. ISBN 978-1-57392-979-0.

81. Old and Middle Kingdom Egypt, Sumerian and Old Babylonian Mesopotamia, Vedic India, pre-Buddhist China, and pre-Columbian Mesoamerica

82. Shushan, Gregory (2009). Conceptions of the Afterlife in Early Civilizations: Universalism, Constructivism, and Near-Death Experience. London: Continuum. ISBN 978-0-8264-4073-0.

83. Schlieter, Jens (2018-08-06). What Is it Like to Be Dead?: Near-Death Experiences, Christianity, and the Occult. Oxford University Press. p. 91. ISBN 978-0-19-088885-5.

FURTHER READINGS

Alcock, James (1979). "Psychology and Near-Death Experiences." Skeptical Inquirer. 3: 25–41.

Lee Worth Bailey; Jenny Yates. (1996). The Near-Death Experience: A Reader. Routledge. ISBN 0-415-91431-0

Blackmore, Susan (2002). "Near-Death Experiences." In Shermer, Ed. M. (ed.). The Skeptic Encyclopedia of Pseudoscience. Santa Barbara, CA.: ABC-Clio. pp. 152–157. ISBN 9781576076538.

Choi, Charles Q. (12 September 2011). "Peace of Mind: Near-Death Experiences Now Found to Have Scientific Explanations." Scientific American.

Carroll, Robert T. (12 September 2014). "Near-death experience (NDE)." The Skeptic's Dictionary. Retrieved 21 August 2017.

Engmann, Birk (2014). Near-death experiences: heavenly insight or a human illusion? Imprint: Springer. ISBN 978-3-319-03727-1.

Bruce Greyson, Charles Flynn. (1984). the Near-Death Experience: Problems, Prospects, Perspectives. Springfield. ISBN 0-398-05008-2

Perera, Mahendra; Jagadheesan, Karuppiah; Peake, Anthony, eds. (2012). Making sense of near-death experiences: a handbook for clinicians. London: Jessica Kingsley Publishers. ISBN 978-1-84905-149-1.

Roberts, Glenn; Owen, John (1988). "The Near-Death Experience." British Journal of Psychiatry. 153 (5): 607–617. doi:10.1192/bjp.153.5.607. PMID 3076496. S2CID 36185915.

Shermer, Michael (1 April 2013). "Proof of Hallucination." Scientific American. 308 (4): 86. Bibcode: 2013SciAm.308d.86S. doi: 10.1038/scientificamerican0413-86. PMID 23539795.

Woerlee, G.M. (May 2004). "Darkness, Tunnels, and Light." Skeptical Inquirer. 28 (3).

Woerlee, G.M. (2005). Mortal minds: the biology of near-death experiences. Amherst, NY: Prometheus Books. ISBN 978-1-59102-283-1.

Lommel, Pim van (2010). Afterlife: a scientific approach to near-death experiences (1st ed.). New York: HarperOne. ISBN 978-0-06-177725-7.

Schlieter, Jens (2018). What is it like to be dead? : Near-death experiences, Christianity, and the Occult times (Hardcover ed.). New York: Oxford University Press. ISBN 978-0-19-088884-8.

Zaleski, Carol (1987). Otherworld journeys: accounts of near-death experience in medieval and modern times (Paperback ed.). New York: Oxford University Press. ISBN 978-0-19-503915-3.

Life After Death

—OUR JOURNEY CONTINUES...—

Chapter 6

GRIEF & GRIEVING

rief is the natural reaction to loss. According to the Mayo Clinic, grief is a strong, sometimes overwhelming emotion for people, regardless of whether their sadness stems from the loss of a loved one or a terminal diagnosis they or someone they love to have received. They might feel numb and removed from daily life, unable to continue with regular duties while saddled with their sense of loss. Grief is both a universal and a personal experience. Individual experiences of grief vary and are influenced by the nature of the loss. Some examples of loss include the death of a loved one, the ending of an important relationship, job loss, loss through theft, or the loss of independence through disability. Experts advise those grieving to realize they can't control the process and to prepare for varying stages of grief. Understanding why they're suffering can help, as can talking to others and trying to resolve issues that cause significant emotional pain, such as feeling guilty for a loved one's death.

Mourning can last for months or years. Pain is tempered as time passes, and the bereaved adapts to life without a loved one, to the news of a terminal diagnosis, or to the realization that someone they love may die.

The Mayo Clinic [1] further suggests that you consult your healthcare professional if you're uncertain whether your grieving process is normal. Outside help is sometimes beneficial to people trying to recover and adjust to a death or diagnosis of a terminal illness.

"One of the most commonly known theories about grief is that we go through 'stages,'" says counselor Nathan MacArthur [2]. "But more recent research – and my experience of collaborating with grieving people – would suggest grief is messier than that. We can feel we're starting to become more accepting of the reality of a loss, then unexpected waves of emotions come over us – when we see someone who looks like the person who died, for example, or a particular piece of music comes on." [2]

Grief is a universal experience and can be a response to losses of many types. "All of us experience some loss throughout our lifetimes," says grief counselor Wendy Liu. [3] "These include the breakdown of a relationship, miscarriage, death, divorce, the loss of a pet, losses through changes in the workplace, loss of sexual intimacy, or loss of independence through illness or injury."

American-Swiss psychiatrist Elisabeth Kübler-Ross first highlighted 5 stages of grief in her book, "On Death and Dying," in 1969 and became a pioneer in death and dying. [4]

144

These stages are often called the Kübler-Ross model or the "DABDA" model (an acronym for Denial, Anger, Bargaining, Depression, and Acceptance). Kübler-Ross based her observations on her work with terminally ill patients, but the model has since been applied more broadly to other types of grief and loss. Since

then, her approach has been adapted and extended to 7 stages. What's important to note is that everyone's grief journey is unique. And, while referred to as 'grief stages,' it's important to mention they aren't set in stone: sometimes the stages overlap or are skipped altogether. However, as you experience them, understanding these seven elements can help identify some of the emotions you may experience.

The seven stages of grief (adapted from Dr. Elisabeth Kübler-Ross, 1969)

1. Shock

Feelings of shock are unavoidable in every situation, even if we have had time to prepare for losing a loved one. We know it will happen, but not right then, not on that day. People in shock often behave normally without emotion because the news has not fully sunk in.

"Often there is a sense of numbness and a self-protective detachment from your feelings because they are too intense to deal with." [2].

2. Denial

Many people experience denial after a bereavement: they know something has happened, but it does not feel real.

"For me, the denial was not that I did not believe it – it was more a sense of, 'But how can they not be here? How can they have been here, and now they are not?" [3]

In addition to experiences of shock and denial, people often describe having a 'mental fog,' says Nathan. "This can include forgetfulness, lack of concentration, sleeplessness, lack of motivation, repetitive thoughts, and inability to make a decision."

3. Anger

It is perfectly normal to feel anger in times of loss, but often people try to keep this stage of grief hidden.

"Anger is a difficult emotion to deal with and can be minimized by others. "But it is important to find someone with whom we can connect honestly." [2]

"I felt frustrated that my grief experience differed from those I was close to. I was angry that I was taking too long and wanting to talk about Mum and Dad to people who felt I should have moved on." [3]

4. Bargaining

The bargaining stage is about making promises to yourself or a higher being, asking the universe for a chance to put things right. A bereaved person may seek reason where there is none and may feel guilty about how they behaved or think in some way to blame.

146

"There's a sense, 'Maybe I could have done things differently. "If I'd stopped them from leaving the house or knew more about their medical condition, I could've intervened. We may feel helpless and hopeless and consumed by thoughts of, 'What if?' [2]

5. Depression

The jumble of emotions that usually accompanies the grieving process can typically lead to feelings of depression, isolation, anxiety, and a sense of dread. Sometimes the suffering seems too much to bear. "Someone may question the meaning of life or feel they want to be reunited with the person that's died," In cases like this, it is so important to ask for help.

"People are often unsure of how to help us in our grief, so if you can accept an offer of help or ask for help, it will strengthen those friendships," he adds [2]

6. Acceptance and hope

Humans, by nature, crave contact, connection, and support, and at some stage in the grieving process, they will want to engage with friends and family again. Acceptance is about realizing you cannot change the circumstances but can gain some control over how you respond.

Every story has and end but in life every ending is just a new beginning

"At times, we may need to distract ourselves from the grief or place it to one side to get on with work or social situations" [2]

147

But this is also a stage where you might slip backward and feel overwhelmed by all the emotions again. It is normal to move between any grief stages from hour to hour or even minute to minute.

7. Processing grief

There is no right or wrong way to grieve – the process is highly individual. In addition, there is no quick fix; the healing process takes time and varies from person to person. Importantly, there is no "normal" period, so be patient with yourself.

The following coping strategies may be helpful:

- Express your grief in words or another creative outlet, such as painting or drawing.
- Connect with others – this can be loved ones or community support groups.
- Ask for help in whatever form.
- Practice deep breathing regularly.
- Set small, realistic goals.
- Ensure you get enough sleep and aim for movement each day.
- Eat a healthy, balanced diet and keep hydrated.
- Rehearse how you respond to questions and new situations.
- Getting help with grief. [3]

(Ed.: Given the distress and pain grief and grieving creates, the author has included additional information from a different specialist grief counselor. Note: any information provided should not be taken as a substitute for individual professional advice).

148

Effect on a child in the loss of a loved one. [5] [6]

Losing a loved one can be an incredibly difficult experience for anyone. Still, it can be particularly challenging for children who may not fully understand the concept of death or have the emotional maturity to process their grief. There are several ways for a caregiver to support a child who is grieving:

1. Be present and available: Let your child know that you are there for them and that they can talk to you about anything they are feeling. Please encourage them to express their emotions and listen to them without judgment.

2. Provide comfort: Offer physical comfort such as hugs, cuddles, or being physically present. You can also provide emotional comfort by offering encouragement and letting them know it is okay to feel sad.

3. Keep routines: Maintaining normal habits, such as mealtimes, bedtimes, and school schedules, can provide stability and comfort during challenging times.

4. Provide age-appropriate information: Depending on the child's age, provide simple and honest explanations about death and what it means. Avoid euphemisms or confusing language.

5. Encourage self-expression: Allow your child to express their emotions through art, music, writing, or other creative outlets. These can provide a healthy way for them to process their grief.

6. Seek professional help if your child is struggling with their grief or you feel they may benefit from additional support; consider seeking a mental health professional specializing in grief counseling for children.

It is important to remember that everyone grieves differently, and there is no right or wrong way to grieve. The most important thing you can do is provide a safe and supportive environment for your child to express their emotions and work through their grief in their way and at their own pace.

What do you tell a child who asks about the afterlife after losing a loved one? [7]

Talking to a child about the afterlife after losing a loved one can be a sensitive and personal topic. Here are some tips and resources to help guide you in these conversations:

1. Be honest: It is important, to be honest with the child while considering their age and level of understanding. Let us share that people have different views on what happens when a loved one dies. Perhaps share that people have different beliefs. Many believe your loved ones can still be around to help and love you, although you cannot see them. All the major religions believe in and support the view of an afterlife.

2. Use age-appropriate language: Use language appropriate for the child's age and level of understanding. Avoid using euphemisms or confusing language that may lead to more questions.

3. Respect their beliefs: If the child has a particular religious or cultural belief, respecting their opinions and providing consistent information is important.

4. Offer comfort: Offer words of comfort and reassurance, emphasizing that the loved one will always be remembered and cherished, even if they are no longer physically present.

5. Use books and resources: Many books and resources help parents and caregivers navigate these difficult conversations with children. Some popular ones include: "Lifetimes: The Beautiful Way to Explain Death to Children" by Bryan Mellonie and Robert Ingpen, "The Invisible String" by Patrice Karst, and "When Someone Very Special Dies: Children Can Learn to Cope with Grief" by Marge Heegaard.

Remember that grief is a personal and individual experience. It is important to provide support and understanding to children as they process their emotions and face losing a loved one.

If someone you love is in a state of grief, don't hesitate to get help and support from a professional health provider or psychologist; there are also specialist grief counselors with expertise in providing support and showing a way forward in handling emotional pain.

Author's Comment

In our life, we will no doubt experience, at some time, the loss of a loved one. Even as a child, we often learn the pain of losing someone we love. It may be a lost pet, an aunt or uncle, a grandparent, or someone else who is loved. Many parents will counsel their child by suggesting "... they have gone to Heaven" even if the parents don't believe in Heaven themselves, as it provides some comfort to the pain. "Gone to a better place" is probably a poorly placed suggested alternative, as what could be "better" than being where they were – alive and among those who love them?

This author suggests one may never get over it (the loss), but with help, guidance, love, and support – there is the opportunity to get through it, which will take time. Living through the pain, albeit a minute at a time, then an hour at a time, progressing after that until the pain of the event softens. No magic or sacred words can be shared with someone grieving to remove the pain - just be there to provide comfort and support. There are good reasons to believe in an afterlife - those that hold this belief can often endure the suffering better, knowing that one day they will be in a loving reunion in the afterlife. The author strongly believes that 'the departed' are not 'gone' but remain close by - bound by love but in a different dimension. More about this is in Chapter 8, Communication.

Poem Memory Of A Loved One

A heavy heart, a weight of grief

The pain of loss is beyond belief.

A loved one is gone, but memories stay.

The ache inside won't go away.

Tears flow freely with each thought.

A life cut short; the battle fought.

A void left that can't be filled

A heart that's shattered, a soul that's chilled.

Yet, in the pain, a glimmer shines

A love that's pure and always aligns.

A connection that death can't sever.

A bond that lasts forever and ever.

So, grieve, my friend, and take your time.

For healing comes in its own sweet rhyme.

Remember the love, the joy, the laughter.

And hold them close forever after.

Life After Death

— OUR JOURNEY CONTINUES... —

Sources

1. *https://www.mayoclinic.org/patient-visitor-guide/support-groups/what-is-grief*
2. *Shonagh Walker and Sara Mulcahy, May 2022*
3. *https://www.hcf.com.au/health-agenda/body-mind/mental-health/moving-through-grief*
4. *Kübler-Ross, Elisabeth. (1969) "On Death and Dying."*
5. Child Mind Institute. (n.d.). Talking to Kids About Death. Retrieved from https://childmind.org/article/talking-to-kids-about-death/
6. National Alliance for Grieving Children. (n.d.). Talking to Children About Death. Retrieved from https://childrengrieve.org/talking-children-about-death
7. Verywell Family. (2020). How to Talk to Kids About Death and Dying. Retrieved from https://www.verywellfamily.com/how-to-talk-to-kids-about-death-and-dying-1094798

Additional Reading:

1. "Lifetimes: The Beautiful Way to Explain Death to Children" by Bryan Mellonie and Robert Ingpen.
2. "The Invisible String" by Patrice Karst.
3. "When Someone Very Special Dies: Children Can Learn to Cope with Grief" by Marge Heegaard.

— OUR JOURNEY CONTINUES... —

Chapter 7

WHAT HAPPENS WHEN YOU DIE?

INTRODUCTION

It is a sad time when a person dies. Relatives and friends gather to mourn and offer condolences. When a person dies, the body begins to rot. But how did this happen? Many people wonder what happens to people after they die. Many religions have different ideas about what happens to a person after death. Most religions hold that people's souls go to the afterlife when they die. Based on this belief, they perform the last rites to allow their souls to reach the afterlife. They also serve these rituals according to their religious beliefs so that their souls can be saved. Egyptian religion had multiple opinions about when a person dies. They believed that when a person died, their soul passed into the afterlife, where Osiris, the god of justice, would judge them. They believed that if he did something evil, his soul would be punished, but if he did something good, his soul would be rewarded. The Bible reported that Jesus died on the cross and then did rise from the dead three days later based on passages in Matthew 28:6 and John 20:17. That Jesus died on the cross as a savior to humankind to forgive the sin of humanity.

What happens to the body after death?

When someone dies, a range of deathly changes occurs in the body. Brain stem death causes cardiovascular, respiratory, endocrine, metabolic, and hematological changes.

The body is a tangible reminder of one's mortality, and its fate after death is important to many cultures, societies, and individuals. After death, the body may be treated ritualistically to transition the deceased from the realm of the living to that of the ancestors [3]. This ritual may involve treatments such as embalming, washing, and dressing the body [3]. In addition, mortuary ceremonies may occur after social and physical death [3]. Social death occurs when the body is considered to have died and ceased functioning for life [3]. It can happen before or after physical death, and several studies have used the concept of social death to reflect on how people can be treated as if they are already dead within clinical and social care settings.

The decomposition process is the natural breakdown of organic matter, beginning immediately after death [4]. Depending on the environmental conditions, this process can take days, months, or even years to complete [4]. It is divided into five stages: Fresh, Bloated, Decay, Postdecay, and Skeletal [5]. During the Fresh stage, the body remains intact [4] and is consumed by insects [6]. The Bloated stage is when the body begins to swell due to the accumulation of gases [4]. During the Decay stage, the body decomposes, and the soft tissue breaks down [4]. This is followed by the Postdecay stage, where the body begins to dry out, and the skin begins to shrink [4]. The final stage is Skeletonization, which may take hundreds of years for the last bone tissue and mineral phases to disappear [4]. Law enforcement personnel often use insects, mites, and other arthropods to estimate the post-mortem interval [5]. Traditional post-mortem interval estimates are based on observations of changes to the body, such as livor mortis, algor mortis, and rigor mortis [5]. Decomposition in xerophytic habitats can be slower than in contact with the soil [6], and humus decomposition occurs due to the breakdown of organic matter [7]. The

157

decomposition process is complex and varies depending on the environment [4].

Immediately after people die, their bodies rot and decompose unless they are preserved with chemicals. The human body comprises many organs that work together to maintain homeostasis in our body. When a person dies, their body stops receiving stimuli from the brain and senses; therefore, all his organs stop working. This causes all its organs to decay simultaneously, causing the body to rot and decompose. After death, bacteria in the digestive system eat away at the internal organs until only the bones remain. The body then begins to change into a liquid form as it breaks down until only the bones remain - unless preserved with chemicals or cremated after preservation. According to Dr. George Rodonaia, MD, PhD., doctors can now tell when a person is dying before they die by detecting specific changes in heartbeat and blood pressure. Doctors call this process "vital sign monitoring" or "vital sign assessment, and it is a common medical practice in which doctors routinely measure a patient's vital signs, such as blood pressure, heart rate, respiratory rate, temperature, and oxygen saturation to assess their overall health and identify any signs of distress or deterioration."

What happens to the soul (or spirit) when you die?

Different religions have their views on what happens to the soul after death. For example, in Christianity, the soul is believed to pass into Heaven or Hell, depending on its actions and beliefs during life [8]. In Islam, souls are judged by Allah and then sent to either Heaven (Paradise) or Hell.

Religious beliefs dictate what happens to the soul after death, which can help provide comfort and hope to those facing the end of their lives. Judaism teaches that the soul passes on to the World to Come, a place of spiritual reward based on the individual's righteousness in life [8]. Buddhism believes in reincarnation, where the soul is reborn in a different body after death. Hinduism also believes in reincarnation, but the soul is said to cycle through a cycle of death and rebirth until it reaches a state of spiritual enlightenment. These beliefs can provide comfort and solace to those facing death, as they can hope that their souls will be rewarded after death [8]. These matters are reviewed in Chapter 4 of this book.

The Abrahamic tradition, which includes Judaism, Christianity, and Islam, views the transition from life to the afterlife in a specific way. According to this tradition, people who die go to either Heaven or Hell and those who go to Hell will suffer forever [9]. Moreover, those who go to Hell will be reunited with family members who have already possibly also gone to Hell. In contrast, those who go to Heaven will live on Earth and be reunited with family members who have already gone to Heaven [9]. The Abrahamic tradition also views dreams as communicating with God to understand the present and predict the future [10]. Specifically, the unidirectional destination of the God-centered view is that the soul will ascend to well-articulated Heaven after death, become united with a divinity

[9], or descend to Hell. This contrasts the cosmic-spiritual view, which reflects certain ideas in non-Abrahamic religions such as Buddhism and Hinduism and assumes a less narrowly defined destiny [9].

Eastern traditions have long embraced the notion of a life after death, from the ancient Chinese to the modern-day Hindus. In these spiritual traditions, the transition from life to the afterlife is seen as an ongoing cycle of life and death, with the soul reborn into a new life after death. This belief has been passed down through generations and is still a fundamental part of many Eastern spiritual practices today. The idea of reincarnation, or the cycle of rebirth, is especially prominent in Hinduism. According to the Hindu faith, the soul is reborn into a new body after death, and the previous life's karma, or deeds, determine the quality of the next life. In Buddhism, the cycle of death and rebirth is known as samsara, and the soul is believed to be reborn until it reaches spiritual enlightenment. Furthermore, according to Taoism, the soul is believed to be reborn into a new life until a state of perfect harmony or oneness with the universe comes. This concept of reincarnation is an integral part of the Eastern spiritual tradition and is believed to be the key to understanding the mysteries of life and death.

Every story has and end
but in life every ending
is just a new beginning

There is much to learn about death and what happens afterward. Recent research in quantum physics suggests that death may not be the end but rather a transition to a higher state of being. If this is true, it means that death is not necessarily a terrible thing, merely a continuation of the cycle of nature which will occur to everyone. The study suggests that death is not the ultimate destination but simply a stop on a journey. Many believe our consciousness lives on after death and is transferred to a higher level. This could mean that we are entering a new realm of being, in a spiritual realm. This spiritual realm is a pure state of consciousness, free from physical limitations and full of infinite possibilities. Or it could mean that our consciousness is recycled and used for other purposes. For centuries, this idea of a spiritual realm has been discussed in various religious and philosophical contexts. From a scientific evidence perspective, it is important to note that there is no conclusive scientific evidence to suggest that death leads to a higher state of being or an afterlife. While quantum physics has brought about many fascinating and ground-breaking discoveries, it is still a highly theoretical field operating on the subatomic world level. It has yet to be applied to macroscopic phenomena like life and death. Some researchers have explored the possibility of consciousness beyond physical death through quantum mechanics. For example, physicist Roger Penrose and anesthesiologist Stuart Hameroff have proposed a theory of quantum consciousness, which suggests that consciousness arises from the quantum-level activities of microtubules in the brain. They suggest that these quantum processes may continue after death, allowing consciousness to persist in some form.

Another theory, known as the many-worlds interpretation of quantum mechanics, proposes that every decision or event splits the universe into multiple parallel realities, each with its version of events. In this view, death may be seen as a transition from reality to another rather than the end of existence.

The concept of reincarnation is more deeply explored in Chapter 4 of this book. It suggests that when a person dies, their soul is reborn in another body, either in the same or future life. This idea of reincarnation is based on the belief that life is circular and that everyone is a spiritual being with a deep connection to the universe. According to this, death is not the end of life but a new beginning. The soul is believed to be reborn in a different form, with a new identity and purpose. Hindus believe the state can be a person, an animal, or even an element in nature. In this way, the soul is believed to continue its eternal journey, learning, and growing with each new life.

When a person dies, the soul is believed to embark on a journey to the afterlife. Depending on the religion or belief system, the soul may undergo a purification process, and rewards can be given based on actions taken in life. The soul's journey is believed to be guided by spiritual beings such as angels or other deities. This spiritual presence helps the soul navigate the afterlife and find its destination. Depending on the belief system, this could be a place of peace, contentment, judgment, and punishment. Eventually, the soul will reach its final resting place. This resting place is believed to be where the soul dwells eternally, within peace or, depending on its actions in life.

Most religions suggest an afterlife is a place of hope and reward (conditional and exclusively for parochial followers of their faith). It is common for believers in the afterlife to believe that their souls will be judged after death based on the good deeds they did in life and the way they lived. Religions prophesize that when people do enough good deeds, they will get a place in Heaven to spend eternity in happiness and peace (again, conditional on parochial 'followship' while in the living). For those who are evil, it is also commonly believed they are sent to Hell, a place of eternal suffering and torment (see Chapter 3 of this book).

Unbelievers believe that death marks the end of a person's life and that there is nothing after death. They believe that when a person dies, their body deteriorates, and their memories of them fade over time. There is no life after death, judgment, reward, or punishment. Instead, those who knew them can remember them uniquely, and their legacy lives on through the works they created and the people they influenced. But many other beliefs offer different views of what happens to a person after they die. As mentioned, Hindu religions and spiritual practices believe that a person's soul continues to exist in some form, either in an afterlife or in a new life form. They believe that a person's actions in life determine what happens to his soul after death. Other beliefs may involve reincarnation or the belief that one's soul is reborn in another body.

The Findings of Emanuel Swedenborg

Emanuel Swedenborg was an 18th-century Swedish scientist, philosopher, theologian, and mystic who claimed to have had a series of mystical experiences that led him to write extensively on spiritual and metaphysical topics. His writings influenced various religious and philosophical movements, including 'Swedenborgianism,' the New Church, and Transcendentalism *(Transcendentalism is one of the first philosophical currents that emerged in the United States; it is, therefore, a key early point in the history of American philosophy. Emphasizing subjective intuition over objective empiricism, its adherents believe individuals can generate original insights with little attention and deference to past masters. It arose as a reaction to protest intellectualism and spirituality at the time. The doctrine of the Unitarian church, as taught at Harvard Divinity School, was closely related).*

Swedenborg's mystical experiences began in the 1740s when he claimed to have had a vision in which he was visited by Christ, who revealed to him the spiritual meaning of the Bible. From then on, Swedenborg claimed regular contact with spirits and angels and wrote extensively on many spirituality-related topics, including the afterlife, God, the nature of reality, and the spiritual hierarchy.

Swedenborg's work was controversial during his lifetime and has continued to generate debate and interest among scholars and practitioners of various religious traditions. Some have viewed Swedenborg's mystical experiences and teachings as visionary and deeply insightful, while others have criticized his work as unorthodox, speculative, or even heretical. Nevertheless, Swedenborg's writings have had a lasting impact on religious and philosophical thought, and his ideas continue to influence spiritual seekers and scholars worldwide. His body of works of Heaven, Hell, and the afterlife is extensive and well-published and debated for decades since his death. There is no doubt of his reputation for invention and scientific discovery, and he was extremely well regarded, especially in Sweden. He had an almost Leonardo Da Vinci level of respect as a scientist. He placed his reputation on the line as a renowned scholar by reporting the findings of his spiritual experience in the afterlife and is worthy of a voice in this book. For the purpose of academic review and study, a minuscule number of extracts from his research are reproduced below relevant to the research question of this chapter. *(Ed. Where bold lettering is used in the text or citation, the author has inserted this to add emphasis).*

All rights and copyright of the following extracts and citations remain the property of the Swedenborg Foundation and are reproduced with their kind permission. The author recommends that readers interested in this subject area should view www.swedenborg.com

What the World of Spirits Is

The world of spirits is neither heaven nor hell but a place or state between the two. It is where we first arrive after death, being in due time either raised into heaven or cast into hell from it, depending on our life in this world. The world of spirits is halfway between heaven and hell and our own halfway state after death. There is a vast number of 'people' in the world of spirits because that is where everyone is first gathered, examined, and prepared. There is no fixed limit to our stay there. Some people barely enter it and are promptly either taken up into heaven or cast down into hell. Some stay there for a few weeks, some for many years, though not more than thirty. The variations in the length of stay occur because of the correspondence or lack of correspondence between our deeper and our more outward natures.

Source: The World of Spirits and Our State after Death. Page 3).

After we die, just as soon as we arrive in the world of spirit, we are carefully sorted out by the Lord. Good people are immediately connected with the heavenly community because their love, thoughtfulness, and faith are affiliated with them within the world. Evil people are immediately connected with the hellish community because their ruling love is affiliated with them within the world.

(Source: The World of Spirits and Our State after Death, page 3).

Even though we are sorted out this way, we are still together in that world and can talk to anyone when we want to, to friends and acquaintances from our physical life, especially husbands and wives and siblings. I have seen a father talking with his six sons and recognizing them. I have seen many other people with their relatives and friends. However, since they were different because of their life in the world, they parted company after a little while. However, people coming into heaven from the world of spirits and those coming into hell do not see each other anymore. They do not even recognize each other unless they are like because of a likeness in love. They see each other in the world of spirits but not in heaven or hell because they are brought into states like the ones they were in during their physical lives, one after another. After a while, though, they settle into a constant state that accords with their ruling love. On these pages, where it says "spirits," it means people in the world of spirits, while "angels" means people in heaven. In this state, mutual recognition comes only from the similarity of love, for likeness unites, and difference separates.

(Source: The World of Spirits and Our State after Death, page 4).

We need to realize that the only way of controlling the violent rage of people in the 'Hells' is through fear of punishment. There are no other means. **The Lord does not cast anyone into Hell: spirits cast themselves. Some people cherish the notion that God turns his face away from people, spurns them, and throws them into Hell ...Some go as far as to think that God punishes people and does them harm.** They support this notion from the literal meaning of the Word where things like this are said, not realizing that the spiritual significance of the Word, which makes sense of the letter, is different. So, the real doctrine of the church, which is from the spiritual meaning of the Word, teaches something else. **It teaches that the Lord never turns his face away from anyone, spurns anyone, casts anyone into hell, or** is angry. **Anyone whose mind is enlightened perceives this while reading the Word simply because the Lord is goodness, love, and mercy.** Good itself cannot harm anyone. Love and compassion cannot spurn anyone because this is contrary to mercy and love and is, therefore, contrary to divine nature.

Source: The World of Spirits and Our State after Death, page 5).

When we arrive in the other life, we are first taken up by angels who do everything for us, tell us about the Lord, heaven, and divine life, and offer us lessons in what is good and true. However, if we as spirits are the kind of people who have been familiar with things like this in the world but have denied or rejected them at heart, then after some conversation, we want to get away from them and try to leave. When the angels notice this, they leave us. After spending time with various other people, we eventually accept people devoted to similar evils. When this happens, we are turning away from the Lord and turning our faces toward the Hell we were united in the world, where people are engaged in a similar love of sinful life. We can see from this that the Lord is leading every spirit toward himself through angels and an inflow from heaven. However, spirits absorbed in evil resist strenuously and virtually tear themselves away from the Lord. They are drawn by their evil - by Hell, that is, as though it were a rope, and because they are removed and want to follow because of their love of sin, it follows that they freely cast themselves into Hell.

Source: The World of Spirits and Our State after Death, page 6).

There are more extracts and research findings from Emmanuel Swedenborg in the later chapters of this book.

Author's Comment

Chapter 5 covered the phenomenon of near-death experiences (NDE). There have now been over fifty years of dedicated scientific studies which have evaluated thousands of NDE cases. The field has progressed from once considered a pseudoscience to a respectable field of study at universities. There is overwhelming evidence to support the argument that there is life after death which has tremendous implications for humanity. Once we pass away, we continue, albeit in a different dimension and a spiritual state. Most of the world's major religions have scaffolded their belief systems upon the precept that there is life after death, so these findings should be hardly surprising. It is perhaps disappointing that most of the major religions also predicate their dogma to include that passage into Heaven, Paradise, or Nirvana through observing the teachings of their particular faith. This author suggests that there are more relevant determinates than which religion one follows. This controversial topic is addressed in Chapter 10.

This author has been quietly an active observer and anecdotal researcher for fifty years across psychic activities; it does not make him any expert nor claim any extraordinary gifts or talents; rather, at best, he is merely an honest broker ready to share some of his findings. As a result, he has formed his views on the legitimacy of this fascinating subject area. These will be unpacked in the Conclusion of this book. However, at this juncture, the author shares the following personal revelations.

Revelation One: There is no doubt there is a life after death and living in this physical (or natural) plane is part of the cycle of our preparation for the afterlife. We are all on a pathway of learning and spiritual development. We take a legacy using what we have done, to what we chose not to do.

Revelation Two: Our loved ones who depart from us have not permanently left. They are certainly not (fully) in the cemetery awaiting decomposition (although their physical remains might be if they were buried). Their soul or spirit has long left their body and gone to the afterlife, greeted by loved ones waiting to welcome them. The ones who departed will also be a little sad to leave their living loved ones behind. However, they are often overwhelmed and delighted when they 'see and learn' the big picture. They now know that one day you will all be united.

Revelation Three: Your loved ones will be with you from spirit, still loving and caring for those left behind. They may converse with you when you are in deep sleep or when you have trained yourself in meditation to do so. I have observed countless times that within the first three to four weeks of passing, loved ones will often try and let you know they are still around, albeit in spirit. I have personally experienced and reliably reported to me from people I know and trust many examples of communication, most are subtle, but other cases have been a lot more demonstrative. Refer to Chapter 8 of this book, Communication, for further information and examples.

Revelation Four: The absolute places of Heaven and Hell have been widely misunderstood and do not exist as a single 'and final places' despite the culturing of the idea by early scripture writers. Chapter 3 considered the concept of Heaven and Hell. By our human nature, we have all done wrong things (or thought to do something but didn't), which suggests that even the 'best' of us have sinned and are flawed. Each of us is on a pathway of learning and spiritual development; this is both living in the physical and entering the afterlife.

Sources:

1.https://academic.oup.com/bjaed/article-abstract/12/5/225/289066

2.https://www.jstor.org/stable/3767544

3.https://academic.oup.com/qjmed/article-abstract/110/1/5/2638390

4.https://www.taylorfrancis.com/chapters/edit/10.1201/9781420069921-12/decomposition-chemistry-burial-environment-shari-forbes

5.https://link.springer.com/article/10.1007/s10493-009-9284-9

6.https://link.springer.com/chapter/10.1007/978-1-4020-9684-6_1

7.https://link.springer.com/article/10.1007/BF01343734

8.https://www.sciencedirect.com/science/article/pii/S0140673603133107

9.https://link.springer.com/chapter/10.1007/978-3-030-52140-0_4

10.https://www.frontiersin.org/articles/10.3389/fpsyg.2020.555731/full

Further Reading and Free Downloadable eBooks:

1. "Consciousness and the Universe: Quantum Physics, Evolution, Brain & Mind" by Roger Penrose and Stuart Hameroff (https://www.ncbi.nlm.nih.gov/pmc/articles/PMC5123717/)

2. "The Many-Worlds Interpretation of Quantum Mechanics" by Hugh Everett III (https://www-tc.pbs.org/wgbh/nova/manyworlds/pdf/dissertation.pdf)

3. "Quantum Mechanics and the Consciousness Debate" by Steven Weinberg (https://arxiv.org/abs/quant-ph/0108140)

4. "Death and the Quantum: The Role of Physics in the Understanding of Consciousness" by Derek Abbott (https://www.ncbi.nlm.nih.gov/pmc/articles/PMC6170843/)

5. www.swedenborg.com

6. https://swedenborg.com/bookstore/free-ebooks-downloads/

Life After Death

— OUR JOURNEY CONTINUES... —

Chapter 8

COMMUNICATION

Exploring the validity of communication between the living and the afterlife

Communicating with the afterlife is a belief that people can interact with dead relatives and loved ones after their deaths. This belief is often associated with religious or spiritual practices and beliefs, and many believe in it. However, communicating with the afterlife is controversial because there needs to be scientific evidence to support the idea that people can communicate with the afterlife. This claim is based on faith because it has yet to be proven through empirical investigation. However, anecdotal evidence suggests otherwise, with the turning point towards belief based on one's discovery.

Many people have reported experiences of communicating with the afterlife, which cannot be easily explained. Collectively referred to as paranormal phenomena, these experiences defy rational explanation because they transcend normal physical laws. Many people believe that paranormal phenomena such as telepathy, precognition, and extrasensory perception are ways of communicating with the afterlife. Although paranormal phenomena cannot be easily explained, they cannot be used as evidence for communicating with the afterlife as they are regarded by science at this stage as rooted in pseudoscience and superstition. However, lacking scientific evidence does not mean communicating with the afterlife is impossible or untrue. Although science has yet to prove that humans can communicate with the afterlife, that does not mean it is impossible or wrong since there could be factors beyond our knowledge or control preventing us from doing so. Moreover, if the existence of the afterlife were scientifically proven, there would be no need to have faith or exercise the God-given right of choice.

Dismissing claims of communicating with the afterlife can disrespect those who believe in it and offer comfort to those who have lost loved ones. Some people believe in communicating with the afterlife because they've experienced premonitions about deceased family members or received messages via psychics or mediums. Disregarding these individual experiences can cause emotional distress for those who have lost loved ones and are seeking answers about them after their deaths. By dismissing claims of communicating with the afterlife, we disregard others' beliefs, emotions, and experiences when dealing with death and loss in today's society.

There are many different beliefs and practices when communicating with the afterlife. Here are a few approaches to communication with the afterlife.

1. **Prayer And Meditation.** Many believe prayer and meditation can help them connect with the spirit world. This may involve asking for guidance or communication from loved ones who have passed away.

2. **Mediumship.** Some people turn to professional mediums who claim to be able to communicate with the deceased. Mediums may use various techniques, such as trance or automatic writing, to receive messages from spirits. Another level of mediumship is trance-channeling, which is explained in more detail later in this chapter of the book.

3. **Séances.** A séance is a group gathering where participants attempt to contact the afterlife through a medium or other spiritual practices. Séances have been used for centuries to communicate with the dead allegedly.

4. **Instrumental Transcommunication (ITC).** This refers to using electronic devices such as radios and televisions to communicate with spirits. ITC researchers claim that they have received messages from the spirit world through these devices.

5. **Ouija® Boards.** Ouija® boards are marked with letters and numbers used to communicate with spirits. Participants place their hands on a planchette pointer and ask questions, with the information moving to spell out answers. You can also make your own Ouija® board by assembling a series of letters and numbers under a sheet of glass. You can then use a wine glass in place of the planchet.

Author's comments

Without wishing to appear over dramatic, the author has been an observer or active participant in most of the modalities mentioned in this book for over fifty years as part of his curiosity about learning. Despite science being unable to confirm or deny the existence of an afterlife, and the ability to communicate, he has witnessed and observed many incidences of paranormality which defy rational scientific explanation but are also beyond the reach for inclusion of this book. The author is left with these findings as a critical summary which is also included in other parts of this book under the relevant chapters:

1. There is an afterlife, and one's journey continues beyond the grave. The overwhelming evidence of near-death experiences adds testimony to this.

2. Communication is possible, and your loved ones in spirit can communicate with you, especially in your dreams or during quiet meditation. These abilities can be enriched and enhanced to aid psychic development. If you want to share with a departed one, there is no real value or point in visiting the grave site as 'they' are not there, only their earthly remains. If you feel a strong presence from a loved one, they may already be around. Tune in to your senses, and do not dispel every incident as just being your imagination. These feelings and insights are real.

3. It is also possible to initiate communication with the afterlife, but not always direct with the souls you want, as they are not necessarily on an 'at call' basis.

4. Séances and Ouija® board experiences are surprisingly real but can also be dangerous in the author's view. Many religions warn followers not to engage in such activities for a good reason. When a channel or door to the spirit world is opened, unbelievably, it is like opening your home's 'front door' and allowing unfettered entry. One thing is clear: using the Ouija®

board looks fun, spooky, and attractive, especially to the younger generation. However, the practice is NOT a party game, and its use is not recommended other than for genuine well, conducted sessions. On the one hand, the author has the paradoxical dilemma of having engaged in using the Ouija® board to learn about the afterlife, which is hypocritical by the author, who has gained interesting insights about the afterlife through its usage and recommending for others not to engage. If you must investigate for your discovery, always respectfully and reverently conduct your sessions. Opening and closing prayer is beneficial as it sets the right tone, but most of all, have someone experienced lead these sittings.

How To Conduct A Séance

A séance is a group gathering where participants attempt to communicate with the afterlife. Conventionally any meeting to try and connect might technically be considered a séance. However, the term is more commonly used to refer to using a trance medium, also called channeling. The intention is where the medium allows the spirit to enter their body and speak through the medium as a vessel. It is not recommended to try and conduct a séance without an experienced medium in this type of practice; notwithstanding, these are some basic steps used to perform a séance:

1. Location: Séances are typically held in a quiet, dimly lit room. Total darkness is unnecessary as it only opens the session to use unscrupulous practices by fake mediums. You may want to choose a location with some personal significance, such as a room where the person you are trying to contact used to spend time. However, this is not critical.

2. Invite Participants: Decide whom you want to invite to the séance and, as mentioned, use an experienced medium to conduct the session. There are fake mediums around, so be on your guard for these. One indicator is if the medium is seeking considerable money to host a session (out-of-pocket or small payments are OK). Those who make no charge for sharing their gift demonstrate greater sincerity and integrity to the cause. It is best to keep the group small, usually no more than 6-8 people. Everyone should be comfortable with the idea of communicating with spirits and is aware of the potential risks. Some ground rules should also be set and agreed upon. You do not need only 'believers' to be included but invite those with an open mind that respects the séance process. An openly hostile participant will be counter-productive, and they should be encouraged not to attend.

3. Prepare the Space: Use a quiet location free from excessive external noise or interruptions. Set up a table with chairs in the center of the room. Place candles or other objects on the table to create a focal point (new-style battery-operated candles are a safer option). Turn off any electronics that may cause distractions or interfere with the ambiance. Turn off all cell phones, as these can be a major distraction.

4. Set Intentions: Before beginning the séance, set your preferences and goals. You may want to ask a specific question or seek guidance from a singular spirit. It is important to approach the séance with a positive and respectful attitude and to approach a séance cautiously, being aware of the potential risks. Some people may experience negative or frightening sensations during the séance, and it is important to be prepared for this possibility.

5. Begin the Séance: Once everyone is seated, turn off the lights (or dim them low) and ignite the candles. You may choose to hold hands (or not hold hands) and invite any spirits who wish to communicate to join you. You may want to recite a prayer to create a welcoming atmosphere. This may take ten to fifteen minutes (or more) to gain a response, so be patient. Interestingly, if you conduct, say, weekly or fortnightly regular sittings, after several times, there will be those from the afterlife waiting to communicate.

6. Communication: Participants may begin to feel sensations or hear sounds that indicate a spirit is present. The person leading the session and others participating may also receive insights through clairaudience (hearing), clairvoyance (sensing), or olfactory (sense of smell; for example, recognizing a flower or perfume fragrance). When using the Ouija® board, the planchette or other device will move to the letters or numbers. The users may ask questions and interpret any messages or signs. Remember to be respectful and patient, as it may take some time for communication to start. Using a recording device is strongly encouraged to allow follow-up of messages received, and at times also validating information provided at the séance, which can be later confirmed (this is where many non-believers become bewildered in the integrity of messages received).

7. What can be asked? There appear to be restrictions and limits on subject areas spirits are allowed to discuss when asked directly; however, it is common for a spirit to initiate advice on such matters, but this is always at their discretion.

At any séance or connection with spirit, ask the name of the spirit who communicates with you. Ask questions about them and their life, including when and where they lived, what they did, and if they are happy to reveal details of their passing. They can then be asked why they are making themselves present, whether they have a message to share, and what the news is. The important thing to consider is that the message may not be genuine from the entity they claim to be, or they do not know themselves (being in spirit does not make them 'all-knowing'). If there is a degree of frivolity in how the séance is conducted, you will still contact an entity from the spirit world, but it may not be the type (or character) of the spirit you may want in your house. The key in all seances is 'like attracts like.' All this sounds bizarre and preposterous for the uninitiated; however, after attending two to three genuine sessions, the newcomer is often amazed at what is discovered. In Shakespeare's Hamlet, Act 1, Scene 5, Hamlet (famously says), *"There are more things in Heaven and Earth, Horatio than are dreamt of in your philosophy."*

In this context, Hamlet speaks to his friend Horatio and advises that human knowledge and philosophy cannot fully understand or explain many mysterious and unexplainable things. The phrase is often used to convey that there are many things beyond our current understanding or knowledge and that we should remain open to the possibility of discoveries and perspectives. The study of paranormal activities fits into the category.

8. End the Séance: When the medium feels the communication has ended (say after an hour or so), the medium should thank those from the afterlife who have participated, say goodbye, and close the session.

179

How To Conduct An Ouija® Board Session

The Ouija® board is an albeit primitive way to attempt to communicate with the spirit world through a board marked with letters, numbers, and other symbols. Here are some basic steps to conduct Ouija® board sessions:

1. Choose a Location: these are typically held in a quiet, dimly lit room. Total darkness is unnecessary as it only opens the session to use unscrupulous practices. You may want to choose a location with some personal significance, such as a room where the person you are trying to contact used to spend time. However, this is not critical. Select a quiet, dimly lit place where you will not be disturbed. Turn off any electronics that may cause distractions.

2. Gather Supplies: You'll need the Ouija® board and planchette (pointer). The use of a recording device or note-taker can be useful. A box of tissues will also prove useful, especially when loved ones in spirit come through and identify themselves in revealing certain details or facts no one else knew. You may also want to use battery-operated fake candles or other objects to create a desirable atmosphere; however, total darkness is unnecessary and discouraged.

3. Invite Participants: Decide whom you want to invite to the Ouija® board session. It is best to keep the group small, usually 4-6 people. Make sure everyone is comfortable with the idea of communicating with spirits and is aware of the potential risks. Participants do not have to believe; however, they need to respect the protocol of the process. This is not a party game.

4. Set Intentions: Before beginning the session, set your preferences and goals. Consider discussing among participants what specific questions or guidance are being sought. The session should be positive and respectful, as 'like attracts like.'

5. Begin the Session: You may want to recite a prayer to create a welcoming atmosphere. Everyone sits around the Ouija® board and places their fingers lightly on the planchette (or another moveable device). One person should begin by asking a question or inviting any spirits who wish to communicate to join the session. A common opening call "...is there anyone there?" The planchette or other moveable device will move purposefully and deliberately around the board, sometimes quickly. Once the participants realize no one is pushing the device, attention, and interest are heightened. This is particularly so when the board correctly answers a question to a participant who does not have their finger on the device at the time of the question.

6. Communication: Participants may begin to feel the planchette moving due to spiritual energy. The group may ask questions and interpret any messages or signs. Remember to be respectful and patient, as it may take some time for communication to occur. Do not ask frivolous questions or questions about your financial gain – you might get answers, but they will be wrong.

7. End the Session: When you feel the communication has ended, thank any spirits joining the session and say goodbye. It is important to be respectful and not leave the session open-ended, as this can invite negative energies. Approaching the Ouija® board session cautiously and knowing the potential risks is important. Some people may experience negative or frightening sensations during the session, so preparation is important.

Note: Ouija® is a registered trademark of Hasbro (inherited from Parker Brothers).

WARNING

Officially, no scientific evidence supports the efficacy of Ouija® board use, and some people believe they can be dangerous. Many religions openly oppose any attempt to contact the afterlife by any means whatsoever.

The author does not recommend or endorse the use of the Ouija® board, but if you decide to proceed, you do so at your own risk. Always use your judgment and respect the spirit world even if you do not believe in it.

Over time, you will judge whether there is life after death and whether it is possible to communicate with the departed. For some, it will provide a real awakening about the existence of an afterlife and that contact is possible.

What Is Spiritualism ?

Spiritualism is a metaphysical belief system that has been around for centuries and has been documented in various cultures and religions across the globe. The relationship between spirit and matter is the cornerstone of spiritualism, and the broad metaphysical distinction between these two entities is developed into many and various forms [3].

Mediumship groups exist in various forms of spiritualism. Spiritualists believe that the spirits of the dead survive mortal life and that sentient beings from spiritual worlds can communicate with the living [3]. In addition, they believe that the dead can communicate with us and impart ethical and moral knowledge to the living [2]. This belief system also includes the notion that spirits can be contacted through mediums such as psychics [3]. The phenomena of spiritualism consist of prophecy, clairvoyance, clairaudience, gift of tongues, laying on of hands, healing, visions, trance, apports, revelations, raps, levitation, automatic and independent writing and painting, photography, materialization, psychometry, direct and separate voice [3].

Critics argue that people may want to believe they can communicate with the dead because it means their death is not final. Spiritualism offers a powerful message and an equally powerful answer to life's biggest mystery [2].

All civilizations have seen and recorded spirits since ancient times, and every religion has registered spirit manifestations [3]. Spiritualism is the study of ghosts and their images through physical means such as mediums and objects [3].

CHANNELING (also sometimes referred to as mediumship)

Channeling is a phenomenon that has been practiced for centuries, with evidence of its presence in many different cultures, including the Spiritists in Brazil and Spiritualists in the United Kingdom [4]. It is defined as "The communication of information to or through a physically embodied human being, from a source that is said to exist on some other level or dimension of reality than the physical as we know it, and that is not from the normal mind (or self) of the channel" [4]. Trance channeling is a form where the individual willingly enters a higher degree of trance-like states of consciousness to connect with sources of information outside of ego-awareness [4]. During a typical channeling session, the "channel" sits before an audience and enters a trance state after taking a few deep breaths or chanting a few lines [5]. At this point, the channel's mind is receptive to a particular "spirit guide," which becomes its "mouthpiece." It offers advice and counsel on everything from medical problems to financial investments to improving one's love life [5]. While there is a paucity of scientific information on channeling, what it is, and how it works, a recent survey of 899 people in the United States revealed that 19. 6% of respondents said, "Had a non-physical source from a different level or dimension of reality used your body as an instrument for communication?" [4] additionally, research suggests that channeling-related phenomena continue to be prevalent in contemporary cultures. Some religious groups provide training programs on channeling, and Jon Klimo delivers some of the most comprehensive works on the topic [4]. EEG studies, such as the one conducted by Hughes et al. in 1990, have revealed that channels compared to the controls had greater beta EEG power in all experiment phases and greater theta power on one electrode out [4]. Moreover, research reveals how channeling could work even if one hypothesized that channels relayed accurate information from purported discarnate "beings" [4]. Many media have reported unusual sensory or energetic sensations during channeling sessions, which could be measured using objective measures, such as random number generators (RNG) [4], that may be sensitive to subtle environmental effects associated with shifts in consciousness.

WHAT IS MEDIUMSHIP? (also sometimes referred to as channeling)

Mediumship, the practice of communicating with the dead, has a long and varied history. While it has been popular in many cultures for centuries, it is only in the past two hundred years that it has become popular in the Western world. The term "mediumship" was first coined by Allan Kardec in the mid-19th century [7], and it refers to the practice of communicating with spirits through a medium [6]. There are two main categories of mediumship: mental and physical [7]. Mental mediumship involves the spirits conveying messages to the medium via telepathy [7], while physical mediumship involves the spirits taking over the medium's body and speaking through them [6]. Mental mediums claim to be able to hear, see and feel messages from the spirits. During a typical mediumship reading, the medium passes information from the spirit onto the recipient(s), who is known as the "sitter" [7].

In contrast, physical mediums can produce paranormal physical events such as loud raps, voices, materialized objects, apports, and materialized spirit bodies [7]. Trance mediumship is a form of mental mediumship in which the medium allows the ego to step aside for the message to be delivered. At the same time, telekinetic activity is a form of physical mediumship [7]. Although mediumship is not regarded in a favorable light by traditional Judeo-Christian-Islamic religions, it has seen a recent and dramatic increase in the portrayal of mental mediums in popular culture and a similar rise in practicing mediums offering their services [6].

It's worth noting that the scientific community has generally been skeptical of claims of communication with the spirit world due to the lack of empirical evidence to support these claims. However, some researchers in parapsychology continue to investigate this subject area.

SPIRIT GUIDES

Spirit guides are believed to be spiritual beings assigned to help guide and protect individuals throughout their lives. Here are some steps to discover your spirit guides:

1. Set Your Intention: Before contacting your spirit guides, deciding and being clear about what you hope to achieve is important. State your intent to connect with your spirit guides and ask for their guidance and support.

2. Meditate: Find a quiet and comfortable place where you will not be disturbed. Allow yourself to enter a relaxed and peaceful state. Close your eyes and focus on your breath, clearing your mind of distractions.

3. Visualize: Once meditative, visualize a bright and loving light surrounding you. Ask your spirit guides to reveal themselves and allow any images or symbols to come to your mind. Do not worry if nothing comes to you immediately - trust that the information will come soon. Do not be put off by random thoughts that come to mind from your imagination – some might well be – but with practice, these will become less of a distraction.

4. Pay Attention to Signs: Your spirit guides may communicate with you through signs and symbols daily. Pay attention to any repeated patterns or synchronicities you may encounter, as these could be messages from your guides.

5. Journal: Keep a journal of your experiences and any insights you receive. Writing down your thoughts and feelings can help you better understand your connection to your spirit guides.

186

6. Seek Guidance from a Professional: If you are having difficulty connecting with your spirit guides, you may seek advice from a professional psychic or medium who can help you connect with your guides and interpret any messages or signs. Remember that connecting with your spirit guides is a personal and unique experience, and it may take time and patience to develop a strong connection. Trust in the process and be open to receiving guidance from your guides in many ways.

PROOF

Several studies have been conducted on mediums and their ability to communicate with the deceased, but the results have been mixed and controversial. Some studies have suggested that mediums may be able to provide accurate and specific information about deceased individuals that they could not have known through normal means. In contrast, others have found no evidence to support their claims. One of the most well-known studies was conducted by researchers at the University of Arizona in the 1990s, which involved the renowned medium, John Edward. The study, published in the Journal of the Society for Psychical Research, found that Edward could provide accurate and specific information about deceased individuals he could not have known through normal means. However, the study has been criticized for its small sample size and lack of control conditions.

In 2011, researchers at the University of Arizona and the University of Southampton in the UK conducted a study involving 10 mediums and 10 control participants. The study found that the mediums could provide more accurate and specific information about deceased individuals than the control participants, but the results were not statistically significant.

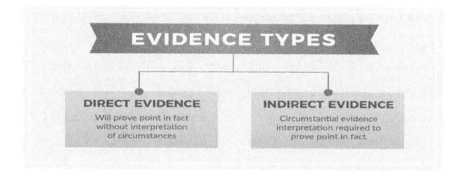

Most of the evidence to support contact with the spirit world and with spirit guides is indirect evidence. It does not make the threshold of being evidenced as a point in fact without interpretation of circumstances.

Other studies have found no evidence to support the claims of mediums, such as a study conducted by researchers at the University of Colorado in 2001, which involved the medium James Van Praagh. The study found that Van Praagh could not provide accurate or specific information about deceased individuals he could not have known through normal means. Overall, the scientific evidence on the effectiveness of mediums is mixed and controversial. More research is needed to understand their abilities better and if and how they may be able to communicate with the deceased.

Additionally, it is important to have realistic expectations and be open to the possibility that communication with the afterlife may only sometimes be possible; also, be aware that you may gain contact with the afterlife but may not be of the character type you wish to converse with.

Example of Contact from the Spirit World

A few years ago, one of the author's past neighbors, Captain Arthur James Hull, Second-in-Command of 'B' Squadron 1st Armoured Regiment as commander of a ready reaction force in South Vietnam in April 1969, was on active duty for one of his many commands during the Vietnam War.

He told me he heard a voice yelling "ground" while trekking through the dense jungle. Jim unmistakably recognized it as his late father's voice and was certain of the event. He immediately went to the ground, as just a few meters away, unseen by Jim, was an enemy Vietcong guerilla hiding in the jungle who sprayed an array of machine gun bullets in an upsweeping motion at him. Jim avoided fatal wounds by taking this evasive action but sustained some injuries which were not fatal. This voice had saved his life! Interestingly, Jim remains steadfast that there is no validity in any life after death, despite his unique experience.

References And Sources

1. Hampton Hill Spiritualists. (n.d.). About spiritualism. Retrieved from https://www.hamptonhillspiritualists.co.uk/about-spiritualism

2. Talk Death. (2021, March 17). History of Spiritualism: Speaking to the Dead. Talk Death. https://www.talkdeath.com/history-of-spiritualism-speaking-dead/

3. Spiritualism (beliefs). (2022, February 19). In Wikipedia. https://en.wikipedia.org/wiki/Spiritualism_(beliefs)

4. Wahbeh H, Cannard C, Okonsky J, Delorme A. A physiological examination of perceived incorporation during trance. F1000Res. 2019 Jan 17; 8:67. doi: 10.12688/f1000research.17157.2. PMID: 30815253; PMCID: PMC6384530.

5. Grace Communion International. (n.d.). Communication with the Dead - Is It Possible? Retrieved March 18, 2023, from https://www.gci.org/articles/communication-with-the-dead-is-it-possible/

6. Delorme A, Beischel J, Michel L, Boccuzzi M, Radin D, Mills PJ. Electrocortical activity is associated with personal communication with the deceased. Front Psychol. 2013 Nov 20; 4:834. Doi: 10.3389/fpsyg.2013.00834. PMID: 24312063; PMCID: PMC3834343.)

7. Mediumship. (2022, March 16). In Wikipedia. https://en.wikipedia.org/wiki/Mediumship

Adapted from the following sources and references on communicating with the afterlife, conducting a séance, and using the Ouija® board:

1. "Communicating with the Afterlife: The Science of Survival" by Jeffrey A. Wands (2005).

2. "Opening to Channel: How to Connect with Your Guide" by Sanaya Roman and Duane Packer (1993)

3. "The Complete Idiot's Guide to Communicating with Spirits" by Rita S. Berkowitz and Deborah S. Romaine (2003).

4. "Séances: How to Conduct Them" by Emma Hardinge Britten (1874)

5. "The Truth about Ouija Boards" by Karen A. Dahlman (2013)

6. "Ouija: The Most Dangerous Game" by Stoker Hunt (1985)

RECOMMENDED FURTHER READING:

"Séances: How to Conduct Them" by Emma Hardinge Britten (1874): This book provides instructions on conducting a séance, a spiritualist practice in which people attempt to communicate with the dead. It covers the phenomena that can occur during a séance, such as a spirit communication and physical manifestations, and how to prepare for and conduct a successful séance. The book also discusses the history and philosophy of spiritualism and the role of mediums in séances.

"**The Truth about Ouija Boards**" by Karen A. Dahlman (2013): This book provides a comprehensive overview of the history and use of Ouija boards, a popular tool for spirit communication. The author explores the myths and misconceptions surrounding Ouija boards and their potential dangers and benefits. The book includes personal anecdotes, experiences from the author and others who have used Ouija boards, and practical advice on using them safely and effectively.

"**Ouija: The Most Dangerous Game**" by Stoker Hunt (1985) explores the potential dangers of using Ouija boards and other forms of spirit communication. The author presents numerous accounts of individuals who have experienced negative or terrifying experiences while using Ouija boards. The book also covers Ouija boards' history, cultural significance, and the psychology of why people are drawn to them. The author offers advice on how to avoid negative experiences and protect oneself while using Ouija boards.

"**Séances: How to Conduct Them**" by Emma Hardinge Britten is a book on Spiritualism and Mediumship published in 1874. The book provides a guide to conducting séances, which were popular gatherings where people attempted to communicate with the spirits of the dead. The book covers diverse topics, such as the history of Spiritualism, the principles of mediumship, the distinct types of spirits, and the preparation and conduct of séances. It also includes detailed instructions on conducting various séances, including physical, mental, and trance mediumship.

The author, Emma Hardinge Britten, was a prominent figure in the Spiritualist movement and authored several books on the subject. "Séances: How to Conduct Them" is one of her most well-known works and is still considered a valuable resource for those interested in the history and practice of Spiritualism.

Life After Death

— OUR JOURNEY CONTINUES... —

Chapter 9

WHAT WILL I DO IN HEAVEN?

POEM – What Angels Do...

In heaven above, where angels roam,

Their duties varied; they have a home.

Their work is pure, their souls divine,

To serve their God, they forever shine.

Some angels sing in harmony,

Their voices sweet, a symphony.

Their hymns reach earth, they bring us peace,

Their music makes our troubles cease.

Others watch over us with care,

Protecting us, they are always there.

They guard our souls, keep us from harm,

Their presence is our lucky charm.

Some angels tend to heaven's gates,

Guiding souls to their rightful fates.

They greet the faithful, welcome them in,

Their kindness, a virtue, never dims.

Their work is endless, their love profound,

In heaven's realm, they are always around.

Their service to God, their eternal goal,

The angels work a permanent role.

Comments by the Author

Given the nature of the question, it is impossible to prove beyond scientific doubt that a spirit, entity, angel, or soul exists and what they might do in the afterlife. For simplicity, the term spirit will be used in this chapter to denote a human who once lived on the earthly plane, who is deceased, and whose soul/spirit went to the afterlife. The term "angel" [5, 6, 7, 8] has its origins in the Greek word "angelos" (ἄγγελος), which means "messenger." The term was later adopted into Hebrew as "mal'akh" (מַלְאָךְ), which also means "messenger." There is ample evidence of angel activity in the Holy Bible, where they have served messages to devotees. There is no reason scripturally why angels cannot continue to visit humanity in modern times.

When a spirit (especially of a past loved one) 'visits' their loved ones in the physical plane, they might technically be termed an angel, given the nature of being a 'messenger from God.' The angel with wings perhaps was an anachronism of times when it was wrongly believed angels lived in the clouds – as it was thought this was where heaven was located.

According to a 2021 survey by the Pew Research Center*, approximately 72% of adults in the United States believe in some afterlife. This includes 58% believing in Heaven or Hell, 22% in reincarnation, and 12% in another perpetuity. (Pew Research Center. (2021). Religious Landscape Study. Retrieved from https://www.pewforum.org/religious-landscape-study) [11]

*These numbers may vary depending on the population surveyed and the methodology used. Additionally, beliefs about the afterlife can be complex and nuanced and may not fit neatly into categories such as heaven, hell, or reincarnation).

No empirical evidence scientifically recognizes an afterlife, nor what spirits might do in Heaven (or that 'other place'). Reliance on such matters is more about belief and faith than science and discovery. Perhaps some issues are so subjective that evaluating them using the scientific method is impossible. Intuitively, as humans, we know there are different types of love. It is personal, similar to other precepts of human existence, such as belief, faith, trust, grief, and love in this category. For instance, there is the love of God (for the religious); love between a parent and a child (and vice-versa); love between a person and their partner, and love between close (but not intimate) friends. The phenomena might all be termed 'love,' but scientifically, proving their differences to an acceptable level of scientific rigor would be difficult.

In the absence of the ultimate - something being scientifically proven, there is reliance on the anecdotal – the experiential, or simply observations over time. From hypothesis to theory, the normal chain of proof of the empirical method leads to evidentiary proof. But this is not the full story regarding research. Some events might be an aberration and dismissed, while other experiences which repeat themselves require closer examination. In short, we should not reject the value of anecdotal evidence but observe, record these events, and critically analyze the data. This meets the criteria of qualifiable research, which can then advance to quantifiable research once the research parameters are defined. The data collected, summaries made, and when these findings become statistically significant critical evaluation occurs. This was the path of enlightenment and discovery of the legitimacy of NDE, where thousands of reported cases were being written, 'begging' more rigorous research to firm up and strengthen the case for life after death. (Refer to Chapter 5 on NDE).

Regarding what a spirit might do in Heaven, to this author, it is inconceivable that a parent who passes over, leaving behind loved ones (be it their child/ren or partner), would not want to remain 'present' in their life, albeit from spirit, to guide and be a guardian angel. The notion of a spirit enjoying life in Heaven in all its beauty, glory, and splendor would be secondary to the desire to continue a loving presence with the loved ones left behind by the grace of God.

Probably the most credible but anecdotal evidence about the 'work' of angels performs comes from the lifetime findings of Emanuel Swedenborg (1668 - 1772), [10]a Swedish pluralistic Christian theologian, scientist, philosopher, and mystic. He was a highly regarded scientist of his era who made several scientific discoveries across various sciences, including geometry, chemistry, metallurgy, mathematical and mechanical inventions, and even had designs for the flying machine. He is also accredited with recognizing the first known anticipation of the neuron concept. He dedicated his research to spiritual matters in his later years and, for over 25 years, recorded 14 extensive volumes, quite extraordinarily, that he had been allowed in his dream state over an extended period to regularly 'visit' Heaven and the afterlife. To conduct interviews and later record his findings. His findings were quite radical at the time, but he wanted to leave as a legacy his work. To achieve this, he completed the study under a nom de plume and made no financial gain from his writings. These have now been faithfully translated from Latin. His findings are surprising and even confronting. Whether the reader does or does not believe its contents, at the very least, will stimulate thoughts about the subject area – additionally, what if he is right in what has been written?

This author shares below some of Swedenborg's observations about the afterlife. Interested readers are encouraged to examine this man's amazing research findings more closely at the Swedenborg Foundation [10].

According to Swedenborg, it is impossible to fully enumerate or describe the various functions of angels in heaven, as each community has its unique role based on its virtues and functions. Everyone in heaven performs specific tasks useful for the Lord's kingdom, founded upon the concept of usefulness. Similar to earthly affairs, there are religious, civic, and domestic services in heaven, with each community differentiated by its particular service form. For instance, some communities are responsible for caring for infants, while others teach and guide children as they grow. Overall, the roles and services in each heavenly society are numerous and varied, determined by their virtues, manifested through their actions and services while in the physical state. Those who have a deep love for their country and its welfare and who act with honesty and fairness because of that love are the ones who are involved in civic affairs in heaven. Through seeking out laws that promote justice based on their passion for service, they gain the discernment necessary to hold positions of governance in heaven, where they perform their duties according to their level of understanding and love for the common good. The number of offices and tasks in heaven is so vast that it cannot be fully enumerated, and those who participate in them do so out of a selfless love for their work and service rather than a love for personal gain or profit. In heaven, there is no love for profit since all necessities of life are provided freely, including housing, clothing, and food.

It is clear that those who prioritize themselves and the world over service have no place in heaven, as our love and affection from life on earth continue to shape our eternal state. In heaven, every individual is engaged in work corresponding to their unique abilities and gifts, with everything reaching a specific use. Engaging in tasks that answer to their use results in a state of life similar to the one experienced on earth but with a deeper spiritual dimension open to greater heavenly blessedness. This spiritual dimension is richer and more profound, creating a more elevated state of being.

Swedenborg suggests that some teach uneducated people from the Christian world and lead them to heaven, and some do the same for various non-Christian people. Some protect new spirits who just arrived from the world from the attacks of evil spirits, and some pay attention to people on

197

the lower earth. Some tend to be people who are awakened from their death. Angels of all communities are assigned to protect us and lead us away from evil *(Ed. ...however, Angels do not override a living person's freedom of choice even though the considered option is abhorrent and evil. Perhaps this non-intervention is why God does not directly intervene to stop bad things from occurring in human life).*

There is no love of gain for a livelihood since all life's necessities are gratified. They are housed gratis, clothed gratis, and fed gratis. We can see from this that people who have loved themselves and the world more than service have no place in heaven. Our love or affection invariably stays with us after our life in the world. It is not uprooted to eternity. Everyone in heaven is engaged in their work according to its 'correspondence.' The correspondence is not with the work itself but with the use of each particular task, and everything has a resemblance. When we are engaged in an activity or a job in heaven that does answer to its use, we are in a state of life very much like the one we were in this world. This is because what is spiritual and what is natural act as one using their correspondence, but with the difference that [after death] we enjoy a deeper delight because we are engaged in spiritual life. This is a deeper life and, therefore, more open to heavenly blessedness. [10]

Angels play a significant role in many religions; their beliefs and functions vary across different faiths. Here are some examples of what some religions believe angels do:

Christianity: In Christianity, angels are seen as divine messengers of God who act as intermediaries between God and humans. They are also believed to be protectors, guardians, and guides. For instance, in the New Testament, an angel is said to have appeared to the shepherds to announce the birth of Jesus (Luke 2:8-14). [5]

Islam: In Islam, angels are considered spiritual beings God created to carry out His commands. They are responsible for recording the deeds of human beings and taking them to God on the Day of Judgment. Angels are also believed to protect and guide human beings. For example, in the Quran, the angel Gabriel is said to have brought revelations to the Prophet Muhammad (Quran 2:97-98). [6]

Judaism: In Judaism, angels are seen as messengers and agents of God. They are believed to be involved in the creation and maintenance of the world. Angels are also supposed to protect and guide individuals and communities. For example, in the Old Testament, the angel Michael is said to have fought against the forces of evil (Daniel 10:13-21). [7]

Hinduism: In Hinduism, angels are known as devas or celestial beings. They are believed to be divine beings responsible for maintaining order and harmony in the universe. Angels are also believed to be involved in the lives of human beings, guiding and protecting them. For instance, in the Hindu epic Ramayana, the monkey god Hanuman is believed to have acted as a messenger and protector for Lord Rama. [8]

Buddhism: In Buddhism, angels are known as devas or celestial beings. They are believed to have achieved high spiritual development through good karma. Angels are also believed to be involved in the lives of human beings, guiding and protecting them. For example, in Buddhist texts, the devas are said to have celebrated the birth of the Buddha and offered him protection and guidance. [8]

Common beliefs as to what angels do in Heaven/Paradise across different religions and belief systems:

Worshipping God: In many religions, including Christianity and Islam, angels are believed to praise and worship God in heaven constantly. For instance, in the Bible, the book of Revelation describes the angels surrounding the throne of God, singing praises to Him (Revelation 4:8-11). [5]

Carrying out God's will: Angels are also believed to act as messengers and agents of God, carrying out His will in heaven and on earth. For example, in Christianity, the archangel Michael is believed to be a warrior who fights against Satan and his demons (Revelation 12:7-9).

Providing guidance and protection: Angels are also believed to offer advice and protection to human beings. For instance, in Islam, the angels are supposed to record the deeds of human beings and protect them from harm.

Serving as caretakers: Some religious traditions believe that angels serve as caretakers for the souls of the deceased in heaven. For example, in Judaism, angels are supposed to accompany the souls of the righteous to heaven after death.

Overall, the specific roles and activities of angels in heaven are believed to be diverse and complex, reflecting the multifaceted nature of their relationship with God and the universe.

This concludes Chapter 9. The next chapter (Chapter 10) considers "What do I need to do to reach Heaven?".

Sources:

1. The Online Etymology Dictionary: According to the Online Etymology Dictionary, the English word "angel" is derived from the Greek word "angelos," which means "messenger." The term was first used in the New Testament to describe the divine messengers who delivered God's messages to humans.

2. Strong's Concordance: Strong's Concordance is a biblical reference work that provides definitions and explanations of the words used in the Bible. According to Strong's Concordance, the Hebrew word "mal'akh" (מַלְאָךְ) is used in the Old Testament of the Bible to refer to both human and divine messengers.

3. Merriam-Webster Dictionary: The Merriam-Webster Dictionary defines "angel" as "a spiritual being that serves especially as a messenger from God or as a guardian of human beings." The dictionary also notes that the word comes from the Greek word "angelos," which means "messenger."

4. BibleHub: BibleHub is an online resource that provides various tools and resources for studying the Bible. According to BibleHub, the word "angel" is used over 300 times in the Bible, primarily in the New Testament. The term is used to describe a variety of heavenly beings, including messengers, warriors, and guardians.

5. The Bible (Luke 2:8-14; Daniel 10:13-21)

6. The Quran (Quran 2:97-98)

7. Jewish texts (Old Testament)

8. Hindu texts (Ramayana)

9. Buddhist texts.

10. Swedenborg Foundation, accessed 31/3/2023 www.swedenborg.com

11. Pew Research Center. (2021). Religious Landscape Study. Retrieved from https://www.pewforum.org/religious-landscape-study) Accessed 23rd March 2023

Recommended Readings:

"Arcana Coelestia" (Heavenly Secrets): Swedenborg's *magnum opus*, a multi-volume work in which he provides a detailed interpretation of the Bible from a spiritual perspective.

"Divine Love and Wisdom": In this work, Swedenborg explores the nature of God, divine love, and divine wisdom and their relationship to creation and human life.

"True Christianity": This book thoroughly examines the Christian faith and its teachings and explores Swedenborg's views on salvation and the afterlife.

"Heaven and Hell": In this work, Swedenborg describes the nature of heaven and hell and explores the afterlife and the spiritual realm.

"The Spiritual Diary" is a collection of Swedenborg's journals, in which he recorded his spiritual experiences and insights.

"The Apocalypse Revealed": This work provides a detailed interpretation of the Book of Revelation from a spiritual perspective.

"Conjugial Love": In this work, Swedenborg explores the nature of love and marriage and provides a spiritual perspective on sexuality and relationships.

"The Doctrine of the New Jerusalem": This book offers a detailed examination of Swedenborg's theology and his vision of the New Jerusalem, a new spiritual age he believed was dawning.

Swedenborg, E. (1749-1756). Arcana Coelestia.

Swedenborg, E. (1763). Divine Love and Wisdom.

Swedenborg, E. (1771-1772). True Christianity.

Swedenborg, E. (1758). Heaven and Hell.

Swedenborg, E. (1747-1765). The Spiritual Diary.

Swedenborg, E. (1766). The Apocalypse Revealed.

Swedenborg, E. (1768). Conjugial Love.

Swedenborg, E. (1763-1769). The Doctrine of the New Jerusalem.

Life After Death
—OUR JOURNEY CONTINUES...—

Chapter 10

WHAT DO I HAVE TO DO TO GET TO HEAVEN?

Salvation according to the Christian faith.

S alvation is a subject that is widely discussed in various religions, and the Christian faith is no exception. The concept of salvation is complex and multifaceted, and it is important to understand the multiple components of salvation [2]. The Bible states that salvation comes only by the grace of God, and there is nothing we can do on our own to guarantee our salvation [3]. Paul also emphasizes moral uprightness; when we fail, we must repent and resolve to do better [3]. Additionally, Paul says we can be justified (made acceptable to God) only by putting our faith in Christ [3].

The Gospel of John emphasizes the importance of believing in Jesus Christ and putting our trust in Him, and it also states that Jesus is the only way to God since no one else claims to be the Son of God [3]. To be saved, we must believe that Jesus Christ—our Lord and Savior—died for our sins and rose again, be willing to turn from our sins and ask forgiveness for our sins [1]. We must also understand that salvation is not automatically achieved when we follow God's commandments and is not a gift given to all [3]. Furthermore, we must acknowledge that justification ends salvation, not the other way around [2], and that justification is the gift by which our sins are forgiven [4]. Ultimately, salvation is the deliverance from sin and its consequences [5], and it is only possible through the grace of God [3].

Difference between mortal and venial sins

Christian theology has long distinguished between mortal and venial sins [9][8]. According to the Catholic Church, a mortal sin violates God's laws and harms one's relationship with Him [7]. When committed, it will result in eternal death [7]. Venial sins, on the other hand, violate God's laws without harming one's relationship with Him [7]. As such, they are forgiven freely and do not lead to eternal death [7]. However, they still weaken one's relationship with God and can lead to more severe sins if not corrected [9]. St. Paul in Galatians (5:19-21) lists several sins that fall into this category [9], such as licentiousness, idolatry, and drunkenness. The First Letter of St. John also mentions venial sin, stating, "All wrongdoing is sin, but not all sin is deadly" [9].

In addition, there are certain circumstances in which sin may be venial, even if it involves severe or grave matters [6]. For instance, if the individual sins without full knowledge or consent of the will, then it may be venial in nature [6]. Thus, it is essential to distinguish between mortal and venial sins [7] and practice regular confession and other spiritual exercises to help form the conscience and avoid grave sin [9].

What does the Bible say about the path to Heaven?

Heaven is a concept that is often discussed in religious circles. The Bible clearly shows two paths to Heaven: righteousness based on works and character based on faith [13]. The latter involves accepting Jesus's sacrifice for humankind, believing he died for our sins [13], and living life for him [12]. Jesus himself is the only way to have an eternal, physical presence in Heaven and eternal life [15]. He is also the only road to Heaven [12][15], so when we're told "narrow is the gate" and "narrow is the way, " we're reminded that many will seek other avenues to Heaven but that the only road that can lead to it is through Christ's sacrifice [12].

The New Testament contains information on what it means to be a Christ follower, with Jesus beautifully detailing and describing "the narrow path" [12]. This path to Heaven is narrow and requires faith in Jesus Christ as the only way to salvation [11], as the thief on the cross had no works to offer before or after his salvation [15]. Salvation is the only way into Heaven [10]. Furthermore, Jesus defines being a Christian as embracing Jesus' sacrifice for humanity, believing he died for our sins, and living life for him [12]. The Bible also states that "Not everyone who says, 'Lord, Lord,' will enter the kingdom of heaven" and that "the one who does the will of my Father who is in heaven" [14] will enter the kingdom of Heaven. Those who do not will be told, "I never knew you; depart from me, you workers of lawlessness" [14].

The pathway to Heaven, according to Judaism

The Jewish perspective on the afterlife is complicated and often ambiguous. The relationships between the immortality of the soul, the World to Come, and the resurrection of the dead often need to be clarified. However, all three topics feature prominently in Jewish tradition [20]. Belief in the soul's survival after death is implicit in the various prayers in memory of the dead and in the mourner's custom of reciting the Kaddish. Orthodox Judaism has maintained a belief in the future resurrection of the deceased as part of the messianic redemption and a belief in some form of the soul's immortality after death [19]. Most Jewish ideas about the afterlife developed post-biblical times [20], which may be connected to the Torah being revealed just after the long Jewish sojourn in Egypt, a society obsessed with death and the afterlife [19]. As a result, Jewish beliefs in the afterlife are as diverse as Judaism itself [18], from the traditional view expecting the unity of flesh and spirit in a resurrected body [16] to the idea that we live on in our children and grandchildren, to a sense of Heaven [18].

The ancients viewed the afterlife as Sheol, a deep and dark netherworld where shadowy spirits called refa'im dwell [17][19]. The Torah has no explicit reference to the afterlife [19]. Still, the concept of resurrection is implied in certain verses. Hence, belief in the eventual resurrection of the dead is a fundamental belief of traditional Judaism, with the righteous being reunited with their loved ones after death [16]. For more information on the wide variety of Jewish views on what happens after death, see Simcha Paull Raphael's book, Jewish Views of the Afterlife [16].

In Judaism, the concept of Olam HaBa, or the World to Come, is a powerful and deeply rooted belief. References to the World to Come can be found in ancient Jewish texts, generally called the afterlife [22]. Olam Ha Ba is contrasted with Olam Ha Ze, which means "this world" in Hebrew [23], and it is believed to be a higher state of being [16]. It is also considered a spiritual afterlife, wherein the righteous dead will be brought back to life and allowed to experience a perfect world [16]. The wicked dead, however, will not be resurrected [16]. This concept of the World to Come is not only a response to the question of what happens after death [23], but it also provides a framework for understanding how one's actions in this world will affect their afterlife [22]. The idea of the World to Come is also a source of hope and comfort for Jews, as it promises an end to uncertainty, miseries, and strife [21]. It is believed that whatever is good in this life will be even better in the World to Come [23]. It is also thought that women will bear children daily in the World to Come, the trees will produce fruit daily, and a single grape will be enough to make a flagon of wine [23]. Ultimately, the concept of the World to Come reminds individuals that their actions in this world have consequences and that their goal should be to strive for righteousness and be worthy of participating in the World to Come [21].

How do Jewish people view resurrection and immortality?

Jewish people view resurrection and immortality in various ways. Orthodox Jewish thinkers believe that the righteous dead will be resurrected in a literal sense, while more liberal Jews reject the notion of resurrection, particularly in its literal form [26]. Conservative Judaism tends to identify resurrection with the doctrine of the soul's immortality, while Reform Judaism has rejected it [26]. This tension between literal and figurative interpretations of resurrection remains in contemporary Judaism.

In the Bible, resurrection is associated with God's mercy and justice [25], and Jewish people believe that the reunion of the soul and body after death is essential for attaining immortality [18]. Other Jewish beliefs in the afterlife include the idea that we live on through our children and grandchildren and the traditional view that the unity of flesh and spirit in a resurrected body is the key to immortality [18]. The Platonic belief that the soul is immortal is also used in Jewish millennialist movements to express the continuity of consciousness after death [25]. The Artscroll prayer book has a line in the bedtime Shema regarding reincarnation [18], and II Maccabees figures the resurrection prominently [19]. The resurrection doctrine is fleshed out in various rabbinic sources, including beliefs that all bodies not already in Israel will be rolled through underground tunnels to the holy land and that during the messianic age, the dead will be brought back to life in Israel [24]. Thus, Jewish people consider resurrection and immortality to be of great importance.

The pathway to Paradise according to Islam

In Islam, Paradise is a concept of ultimate joy and pleasure. It is where the faithful and righteous are rewarded after death for their good deeds in life [28]. The Quran speaks of Paradise in many places, describing it as abundant blessings, with rivers of water, milk, wine, honey, and all kinds of fruits and forgiveness from God [29]. It is also far removed from want, need, anxiety, sadness, sorrow, and regret [27]. The Quran and other Islamic texts also tell us that Paradise is a place that is essentially different from life on Earth, both in terms of nature and the purpose of life, as well as the types of delights people will enjoy therein [27]. Furthermore, it is where one will be offered everything their soul and thoughts desire [27].

God has also shown us glimpses of Paradise in the Quran [27], and Prophet Muhammad (SAW) has said that in Paradise, there are things that are beyond our imagination [29]. Furthermore, Paradise is where one meets and converses with Allah (God) and His angels, sins are forgiven, and enjoys an eternal life of bliss [27]. All of this is a great gift from God and will be offered only to people with whom He is pleased [27]. Indeed, Paradise's reality is something people can only understand once they enter it [27].

In Islam, gaining entry to Paradise is a complex yet rewarding journey. Muslims believe salvation is only through Allah, the Law, and Muhammad [31]. One must be "good" and devoted to Islamic teachings [31]. While this is a more difficult path, there is an easier way to enter Paradise through faith in Allah through Jesus Christ [31]. This is the only way to enter heaven/Paradise in Islam [31]. Allah SWT has made it easy for us to enter His Jannah. However, many of us forget this due to a preoccupation with this temporary worldly life. [31].

To successfully enter Paradise, Muslims must abide by Islamic rules, which outline acceptable behaviors in the Islamic community [31]. By following these rules, all Muslims will enter Paradise [31]. Additionally, anyone who takes a path that leads to knowledge, Allah, the Almighty, will pave his way to Jannah [29]. Moreover, anyone traveling on the road searching for command from Allah will travel on one of the roads of Paradise [30]. Going to the mosque is also a simple way to enter Paradise in Islam [29]. Muslims who go to the masjid purely for the sake of Allah will gain entry to Paradise [29].

Furthermore, Allah will make the path to Jannah easy for whoever takes an approach in search of knowledge [31]. Moreover, whoever meets Allah without ascribing anything to Him will enter Jannah [31]. Additionally, anyone who does four good deeds in one day will enter paradise [30]. According to Islamic belief, many other ways of getting Jannah are not mentioned in this book and are recommended for follow-up [29]

(Ed: my Islamic friends leave with this offering). May Allah Almighty guide us, forgive all our sins, help us stay on the right path, and unite us in Jannah. Ameen! [29]. Lastly, whoever feels like a servant of Allah will enter Jannah Inshallah [31].

Pathway to Heaven for Buddhists - the Eightfold Path and the Four Noble Truths

Buddhism is a religion that is built around the concept of liberation from suffering. This liberation is achieved by following the Four Noble Truths and the Eightfold Path. The Four Noble Truths are the foundation of Buddhism and are the basis of the Buddha's teachings [36]. These truths are 1) The truth of suffering, 2) The truth of the cause of suffering, 3) The truth of the cessation of suffering, and 4) The truth of the path that leads to the cessation of suffering [36].

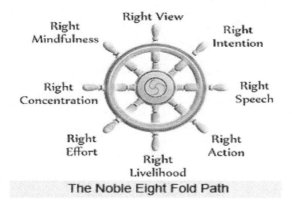

The Noble Eight Fold Path

The Noble Eightfold Path is a set of eight practices that guide people from ignorance of the Four Noble Truths and toward wisdom, virtue, and concentration [32]. These eight practices are Right View [36], Right Intention, Right Speech, Right Action [32], Right Livelihood [35], Right Effort [33], Right Mindfulness [32], and Right Concentration [35].

It is important to note that believing in the Four Noble Truths is less critical than experiencing them [36]. The Noble Eightfold Path is not a set of beliefs or rules but a way of life to be followed and practiced by each individual [32]. It leads to ultimate reality, complete freedom, happiness, and peace through moral, spiritual, and intellectual perfection [32]. The

211

heart of each element of the path is non-clinging, the essence of the Third Noble Truth: the cause of the end of suffering [33]. The Four Noble Truths and the Noble Eightfold Path are the teachings of Buddhism [34], and they shape the thinking of almost all forms of Buddhism [36].

Nirvana is a state of perfect peace and bliss and is the highest aim of human life in Buddhism [38]. It is a state of enlightenment that transcends the sufferings of this world [38]. Nirvana is achieved when one realizes the insight of three universal lakshana (marks): impermanence (anicca), suffering (dukkha), and nonself (anatman) [39]. It is based on the fourfold truths and is explained to mean a state of "without desire, without love, without wish" and one without craving or thirst (taṇhā) [39].

Nirvana can be partially achieved in this life [40] and can also be achieved through self-discipline and practicing the noble eightfold path [38]. In Hinduism and Buddhism, it is the highest state that one can attain and is a state of perfect peace and happiness like Heaven [37].

Upon enlightenment, there is no reincarnation, no rebirth into the cycle of life and death, only non-existence as the suffering self [40]. However, some who have attained enlightenment may choose not to enter the final state of nirvana upon death [40]. Instead, they may re-enter the cycle of reincarnation to continue to help others toward enlightenment [40]. This is because nirvana has more to do with attaining enlightenment or the right knowledge than simply the soul's liberation [38]. It is the middle point of all dualities (Middle Way), where all subject-object discrimination and polarities disappear [39]. The only ultimate reality of emptiness is all that remains, and no conventional reality exists after nirvana since everything is an illusion [39]. Buddha helps liberate beings from saṃsāra by teaching the Buddhist path. His teachings remain in the world for a certain time as a guide to attain nirvana [39].

Significance of meditation, mindfulness, and other religious practices.

Meditation has been a part of spiritual practice since ancient times. It has been used in many religions, such as Buddhism, Hinduism, and Christianity. Buddhist meditation, for instance, has two main goals: mindfulness (the ability to be aware of one's thoughts and emotions without judgment) [41] and gaining insight into reality's true nature [43]. Mindfulness is a polyvalent term that refers to remembering, recollecting, and "bearing in mind"; Buddhist texts mention different mindfulness practices [41]. Hindu meditation, on the other hand, is more about focusing the mind so one can become fully absorbed in union with the Divine [43].

Meditation is a religious practice that benefits mental and physical health and promotes positive social interactions [42]. In Christianity, meditation focuses individuals on their salvation through Jesus Christ and

213

the loving works of God [44]. It involves focusing one's mind on one subject while reflecting on many relationships and aspects of the subject.

Directing and informing one's reflections on the Word of God enhances one's union with the divine [44]. The Judeo-Christian outlook also emphasizes that meditators always maintain their distinct, nondivine personhood while pursuing fellowship with God [44]. In addition, Buddhist meditation traditions also stress self-awareness, detachment, and emotional balance and teach us how to relate to life directly so that we can truly experience the present moment, free from conceptual overlay [44].

Pathway to Heaven for Hinduism

For Hindus, the path to Heaven is a long and arduous one. Since ancient times, two known ways have been acknowledged: the path of piety and righteousness and the path of rituals and prayers [47]. A worshipper can ascend to the divine through great dedication to a particular deity or by understanding the nature of the universe [48].

Achieving salvation (or moksha) requires purification from bad karma [48]. Hindus consider pilgrimage as helpful for one's spiritual development [46]. Many Hindu places of pilgrimage are associated with legendary events from the lives of various gods [46]. The prohibition against killing cows for food is partly due to the belief that cows are the final reincarnated form one attains before merging with Brahma [45]. In Hinduism, Deity does not have an individual personality, it is a force [45], and one who worships God will reach Him.

The Rig Veda speaks of 'pious sacrifices' going to 'the heaven of Indra' in its first book, but it is only in the last book that the idea of Heaven acquires meaning [47]. The various schools of Hinduism have their ideas of salvation, ranging from Advaita's belief that one must strip away the false self and make the soul indistinguishable from that of god to the dualist's insistence that one's soul always retains its own identity even as it is joined with god [48]. In any case, the goal is to experience the beauty of Heaven, where one will find delightful fragrances and comforting sounds, with no aging, sweat or stench, hunger, thirst, heat, cold, grief, fatigue, labor, repentance, or fear [47]. The inhabitants of Heaven will be rewarded with celestial cars and gardens, and the paths that lead to the Siddhas and the Vaiswas will be well provided [47]. To Hindus, the pathway to Heaven is the ultimate destination.

Pathway to Salvation in Mormonism

In Mormonism, the path to salvation is a complex and multifaceted journey. According to Mormonism, perdition, or hell, is reserved for those who resist the church's laws and ordinances [49]. The celestial kingdom is the highest Heaven, and entry into the heavenly kingdom is the goal of the Mormon path to salvation [49].

To gain entrance to the celestial kingdom, Mormons must believe in God and Jesus, repent of sins, be baptized in the church, be a member of the LDS Church, receive the Holy Ghost by the laying on of hands, obey the Mormon "Word of Wisdom" and all God's commandments [48]. Baptism by immersion through a "duly commissioned servant or representative of the Savior" is also required to enter the Celestial Kingdom [49]. This is known as the "gospel" of Mormonism. It is not just a gospel of works but of obedience and obligation to The Church of Jesus Christ of Latter-day Saints [49].

In addition, Mormon doctrine teaches that all people are spiritually dead and must have a savior to be brought back to life [50]. Mormons believe that a person can receive salvation after they have died. They perform acts by proxy for those killed in hopes that those people will convert to Mormonism in the spirit world [50][51].

Ultimately, the Mormon path to salvation is divided into three phases: the preparatory, the transitional, and the celestial [50], and Mormons need to obey the church, its teachings, and the prophet to gain exaltation in the Celestial Kingdom [49].

Pathway to Heaven in Sikhism

In Sikhism, the path to Heaven is found through disciplined, personal meditation on the name and message of God [52]. According to the Guru, Heaven is not a physical destination but rather an experience of living according to the Will of the Lord [54]. Similarly, Hell is not a physical destination but rather the experience of living in ignorance of the Lord [54]. The mission of a Sikh's life is not to get a ticket into Heaven after death but rather to live according to the Guru's teachings and realize the Lord vibrating everywhere in the universe and in every living being [54].

Gurbani doesn't support the existence of Heaven or hell. However, it has mentioned them many times [56]. Ultimately, the final thought at death determines how one reincarnates. Those who dwell on thoughts of riches or worries about wealth are born again as serpents and snakes [53]. Good or bad actions in this life also determine the life form into which a soul takes rebirth [53], and in death, one believes one becomes one with God and the universe [55]. Therefore, life's main purpose is to become one with 5 [55], which is pursued by an energy focused on remembering the Creator always, earning an honest living as a householder, and sharing one's abundance with the less fortunate.

The Authors View

This chapter is bound to cause controversy, so if you are easily offended when a writer suggests an alternative view from your position within your faith, it might be best to skip this next part.

Thank you for reading on. If any offense is caused, please accept my apologies; this is not the intention of this book. In defense, my profession, education, and training as an academic (but new as an author) have instilled contemporary critical analytical thinking - to analyze everything. Only to accept something after questioning. I acknowledge the take-out learning from one of the programs completed at Harvard always to examine "Question Zero," the thinking, reasoning, assumption, or motivation behind asking Question 1. Where are the authors trying to take us when a statement is made? When a message is purported as truth, is it the truth or an alternate 'truth' the authors wish to promote?

I was one of those annoying university students who kept asking why? This probably caused some angst from the other MBA students, except at approaching exam time when I was 'volunteered' by the other students to ask the professors about likely questions in the exam.

My studies have been in business law and business administration - each a long way from theology and understanding the interpretative nuances of ancient texts into contemporary understanding. I rely on religious scholars for their insight into the scriptures, especially those with formal training in theology & philosophy and the courage to ask "why" or challenge the traditional wisdom. Professor Bart D. Ehrman, a Distinguished Professor of Religious Studies at the University of North Carolina, Chapel Hill, is a man of this caliber. In his top-selling book 'Heaven and Hell – A History of the Afterlife.' On the back cover of his book, he opines,

"Where did the ideas of Heaven and hell come from? As strange as it may seem to us now, there was a time when no one thought they would go to Heaven or hell after they died. There is no mention of them in the Old Testament, and Jesus did not believe the souls of the departed were bound for either realm."

(Reproduced with the kind permission of Professor Bart Ehrman. March 2023)

In this watershed book, Professor Ehrman reveals how the concepts of Heaven and hell developed and took hold and why they endure today. He examines the social, cultural, and historical roots of competing views held by Greeks, Jews, and Christians and traces how beliefs changed over time. Ultimately, he shows that many of our ideas about Heaven and hell emerged long after Jesus's time through the struggle to explain the world's injustices.

Jesus did not refer to himself as God.

There is abundant evidence that Jesus did not refer to himself as God. For starters, Jesus did not call himself God or consider himself God [59]. This is further corroborated by the fact that none of his disciples knew he was God [59]. On the contrary, Jesus revered God, His Father, and only saw himself as one part of God's story [60]. Furthermore, the Gospels of Matthew, Mark, and Luke would not mention that Jesus called himself God if that's what he was declaring about himself [59]. On the other hand, the Gospel of John provides a theological understanding of Jesus that is not what was historically accurate [59]. Additionally, the Bible never records Jesus saying precisely, "I am God" [58]. Yet, Jesus claimed to be God without explicitly stating these words [58]. He often pointed to the Old Testament, where he was called God's son. Then he explained to his followers what was said in all the Scriptures concerning himself [60]. Moreover, after His resurrection, Jesus reminded His followers how foolish they were for not believing in Him and all that was written in the Scriptures concerning Him [60].

Additionally, Jesus was often more subtle in displaying His God-nature, making indirect references to his identity with statements like, "I am the way and the truth and the life" (John 14:6, New International Version) or "I am the light of the world" (John 8:12, NIV) [60]. The New Testament also provides eyewitness testimony to the words, actions, and teachings of Jesus that prove his deity [57]. If we do not get the identity of Jesus right, we will die in our sin (John 8:24), and a false Jesus cannot save us [57].

How the early Christians viewed Jesus.

From the very beginning of Christianity, the early Christians viewed Jesus as a divine being [64]. Christology, the doctrine about Christ, is as old as Christianity. Since Jesus is a figure of the Christian faith, there is no difference between "the Jesus of history" and "the Christ of faith" [61]. As Christians contemplated Jesus and his words and deeds after the Gospels were written, the forms of the witness and worship in the Christian communities were also the forms of the narratives in the Gospel accounts [61].

The early Christians believed that Jesus was God and thought of Jesus as being exalted to be divine, based on pre-literary traditions [62]. As they continued contemplating Jesus, they concluded that Jesus was a human being who was made God, a divine being [62]. Later, they even went as far as to say that Jesus resulted from a union between God and a mortal [62]. Eventually, Christians stated that Jesus was a divine being who temporarily became human [62].

To comprehend the early church's faith regarding Christ, we must turn to the writings of the New Testament, where that faith found embodiment [61]. The Apostles' Creed is a later form of a creed that did not achieve its present condition until quite late. Christians told stories about Jesus being born of a virgin and believed that Jesus was the son of God during his entire life [62]. Later, Christians started to say that Jesus was God, the messiah [62], and the very creator of the universe [74]. They also concluded that Jesus became the son of God when God raised him from the dead [62].

A high Christology was present from the very start [64], although Jesus was not omniscient, and his knowledge of secular affairs was essentially limited by human conditions [63]. Jesus acknowledged that he was unaware of a detail connected with his redemptive work. He asked questions to elicit information regarding the site of Lazarus's tomb, the number of loaves he had, and the name of the demented Gadarene [63].

Miracles Jesus performed.

Jesus Christ is remembered for his unusual miracles that spanned centuries and cultures. His miraculous works have been documented in the Gospels of Matthew, Mark, Luke, and John [68], and He continues to help humankind in heavenly ways even today [67]. Jesus performed countless miracles to demonstrate God's power for specific purposes [65], such as turning water into wine, healing incurable diseases, and exercising authority over all realms [68]. Jesus even healed without being physically present [68]. The Gospels also record Jesus raising the dead, walking on water, casting out demons, restoring sight to the blind, healing the sick [66], and recovering a variety of people who had issues with their eyes, ears, mouths, wombs, lungs, bodies, and hands [67]. In addition, Jesus provided forgiveness of sin, reminding us that God is more concerned with healing our souls than healing our bodies [69]. Truly, the miracles of Jesus Christ are amazing, and He changed the lives of everyone around Him, and everywhere He went [68]. (Ed. But was he God?)

Chart 10.1   Pathway To Heaven/Paradise/Nirvana

Christians	Muslims	Hindus	Buddhists	Sikhs	Jews
Faith in Jesus	Faith in the oneness of God and the prophethood of Muhammad	Pursuing the righteous and ethical way of life that includes practicing non-violence, truthfulness, and self-control	The right understanding of the Four Noble Truths and the nature of reality. The right intention of developing good intentions and a desire to follow the path of enlightenment.	Devotion to God and follow the Guru's teachings and instructions. Practice meditation on the name of God (Naaam Simran) to purify the mind and focus on the divine.	One. must observe the Torah - the main text consisting of 5 books: Moses, Genesis, Exodus, Leviticus, Numbers, and Deuteronomy.
Accept Jesus Christ as the son of God	Performing the five daily prayers	Engage in selfless service and doing good deeds without seeking personal gain.	Right speech by speaking truthfully, kindly, and compassionately	Service to others breaks down the ego and purifies the mind.	Do acts of kindness, charity, and compassion to others.
Confess sins, repent, and ask for forgiveness.	Giving a portion of one's wealth to people experiencing poverty and needy	Developing concentration, mindfulness, and awareness through meditation and yoga	The right action of engaging in action activities is ethical and non-harmful	Living an eta virtuous. Be honest, truthful, and compassionate.	Observe the Sabbath and Jewish holidays and fulfilling other religious obligations.
Become in life as Jesus lived.	Fasting during the month of Ramadan	Studying the scriptures which contain the teachings of Hinduism	Making efforts to overcome negative thoughts and behaviors.	Treating all beings equally, regardless of caste, gender, or religion	Repentance is acknowledging wrongdoings, expressing remorse, and making amends.

			Right mindfulness develops an awareness of thoughts, emotions, and experiences.		
Overall, to accept Jesus Christ as Savior, repent sins, and strive to live a life of obedience to God.	Performing the pilgrimage to Mecca at least once in a lifetime	Seeking the guidance of a guru: seeking the direction of a spiritual teacher who can provide advice and support in one's spiritual journey.	Right concentration to focus the mind and achieve deep states of meditation.	I am reading and following the Guru Granth Sahib, which contains the teachings and wisdom of the Sikh Gurus. This is essential to achieve liberation.	Jewish people have no specific concept of Heaven or Hell in Jewish belief; however, they believe the soul continues after death and is judged by God based on the life lived on earth.

Which Way to Heaven, Paradise, or Nirvana?

Comments by Author

The author notes a significant shift in how certain Old Testament events, such as Adam and Eve, Noah and the Ark, and the origin of humanity, are taught in his lifetime. While these stories were once represented as true, they are now often regarded as symbolic or poetic with the advent of science. This shift has prompted the author to question the absolute accuracy of Christian Scriptures and consider the possibility of (perhaps well-intentioned) bias in compiling the New Testament gospels.

At the risk of a backlash from fundamentalist Christians (and the author respects your right to your own beliefs), however, the author has some fundamental concerns about receiving the gospels of the New Testament as being literal truth for the following reasons:

1. **Historical context:** The New Testament was written in a specific historical and cultural context that differs from ours. This context includes the time's language, customs, beliefs, and practices. As a result, some of the stories and teachings may be outside of our modern world.

2. **Translation and interpretation:** The New Testament was written in Greek and translated into many languages over the centuries. These translations may only sometimes capture the full meaning of the original text or may be influenced by the biases and beliefs of the translator.

3. **Authorship and attribution:** Some of the books of the New Testament were written by unknown authors, and others were attributed to authors who may have yet to register them. This raises questions about the authenticity and reliability of the text.

4. The missing gospels of the final compilation suggest the desire to present a fit-for-purpose definitive collection with a result in mind. For example, maybe excluding the Book of Mary was a cultural measure to underplay the role of women in the early church.

5. **Contradictions and inconsistencies:** Several contradictions and inconsistencies within the New Testament make it difficult to take the text literally.

6. **Symbolism and metaphor:** Many of the stories and teachings in the New Testament are intended to be understood as symbolic or metaphorical rather than literal. Taking these passages literally can lead to misunderstandings and misinterpretations.

The author also contents historically, the concepts of Heaven and Hell have been used to instill fear in non-believers and encourage them to embrace Christianity. The author observes that the requirements for entry into Heaven are generally consistent among various religions and share similar values, beliefs, and morality. However, each religion has a specific dogma to attain salvation (refer to Chart 10.1).

Finally, the author suggests that a person's entry into Heaven will not be based solely on their religious affiliation but rather on their character, love, compassion, and how they have lived their life by service to others and ultimately by the grace of God. Perhaps those persons who lived their lives being self-centered and self-absorbed in their power, status, reputation, and riches may not be so graciously received by God compared to those who were in service, love, and compassion to others.

Sources that support these views include academic studies of the New Testament, such as those conducted by biblical scholars and theologians, as well as critical analyses by skeptics and non-religious scholars.

Epilogue by Author

Having a point of common agreement is good in a world of differing views. Suggestively, this point appears for the most part; the religions referred to in this book agree and support the existence of **Life After Death**. Christians refer to it as Heaven and Hell, Muslims as Paradise, and Buddhists Nirvana as the final goal. From this point onwards, each religion takes its parochial path for its devotees to reach Heaven/Paradise/Nirvana.

Being part of organized religion is a practical choice because it can foster all the important ingredients of good character, ethics, and values. Common sense based on a loving and compassionate God would not reasonably favor exclusive entry into Heaven as a reward for choosing the 'right' religion to follow. As an analogy to the words of Martin Luther King, Jr., where he pleads for black children of the future that "...one day they might be judged by the content of their character and not the color of their skin," lyrically applied, that entry into Heaven will be based on life lessons learned, the contribution made to humanity, help to the needy, compassion and love, and living a life of morality and honesty already reflected in the teachings of the world's great religions.

So, live a good life, follow a religion of your choice where you feel most comfortable, and be of service and kindness to others as part of the Natural Law and the Golden Rule. Your chosen religion (or none) can be your vehicle to reach Heaven, but it is not an 'express pass.'

We should all be respectful of each other's differing views and beliefs.

The author thanks you for reading this book, challenging as it may be. However, the author's objective has been served if reading Life After Death provides insight or stimulates reflection.

The author is happy to receive your blogs, or emails, on www.lifeafterdeath.au or email author@lifeafterdeath.au

----

References

1. https://goingfarther.net/basics-of-christianity/salvation/

2. https://binmin.org/christian-salvation-3-stages/

3. https://www.christianbiblereference.org/faq_salvation.htm

4. https://openthebible.org/article/how-i-get-heaven/#:~:text=You%20enter%20heaven%20by%20forgiveness,heaven%20by%20the%20Christian%20life.&text=It's%20always%20true%20that%20where,faith%20alone%2C%20in%20Christ%20alone.

5. https://en.wikipedia.org/wiki/Salvation_in_Christianity

6. https://bismarckdiocese.com/news/what-is-the-difference-between-mortal-and-venial-sin

7. https://reformedbooksonline.com/on-the-distinction-of-venial-mortal-sin/

8. https://www.dummies.com/article/body-mind-spirit/religion-spirituality/christianity/catholicism/mortal-and-venial-sins-in-the-catholic-church-192612/

9. https://catholicstraightanswers.com/what-is-the-difference-between-mortal-and-venial-sin/

10. https://www.crosswalk.com/slideshows/10-things-the-bible-says-about-believers-going-to-heaven.html

11. https://www.gotquestions.org/narrow-path.html

12. https://insider.pureflix.com/prayer-faith/understanding-the-narrow-path-how-to-get-to-heaven

13. https://www.frontiersman.com/faith/are-there-two-paths-to-heaven/article_a5a059ca-672f-11e9-b6c8-fb3152dcfc86.html

14. https://biblereasons.com/narrow-path/

15. https://openthebible.org/article/how-i-get-heaven/

16. https://www.jewfaq.org/afterlife

17. https://www.haaretz.com/jewish/2019-02-07/ty-article/.premium/what-is-the-jewish-afterlife-like/0000017f-e62a-dc7e-adff-f6af424f0001

18. https://momentmag.com/is-there-life-after-death /

19. https://www.jewishvirtuallibrary.org/afterlife

20. https://www.myjewishlearning.com/article/life-after-death/

21. https://www.britannica.com/topic/olam-ha-ba

22. https://www.myjewishlearning.com/article/the-world-to-come/

23. https://www.learnreligions.com/what-is-olam-ha-ba-2076769

24. https://www.myjewishlearning.com/article/jewish-resurrection-of-the-dead/

25. https://academic.oup.com/book/12487/chapter/163189688

26. https://www.religion-online.org/book-chapter/chapter-12-resurrection-as-the-hope-for-personal-immortality/

27. https://www.islamreligion.com/articles/11/pleasures-of-paradise-part-1/

28. https://www.learnreligions.com/definition-of-jannah-2004340

29. http://www.quranreading.com/blog/how-does-a-muslim-get-to-heaven-major-ways-of-getting-to-jannah/

30. https://www.islamquote.com/2017/01/10/15-ways-to-enter-jannah-paradise-in-islam/

31. https://backtojannah.com/ways-to-enter-jannah/

32. https://tricycle.org/magazine/noble-eightfold-path/

33. https://www.rickhanson.net/the-noble-eightfold-path/

34. https://www.buddhistdoor.net/features/understanding-the-four-noble-truths-and-walking-the-noble-eightfold-path/

35. https://en.wikipedia.org/wiki/Noble_Eightfold_Path

36. https://www.gotquestions.org/Four-Noble-Truths.html

37. https://rnavya2012.medium.com/achieving-nirvana-buddhism-a1ed03a0455

38. https://iskcondwarka.org/blogs/moksha/

39. https://en.wikipedia.org/wiki/Nirvana_(Buddhism)

40. https://www.patheos.com/answers/what-does-it-mean-to-achieve-nirvana-in-buddhism

41. https://en.wikipedia.org/wiki/Buddhist_meditation

42. https://mindworks.org/blog/buddhist-meditation-techniques-practices/

43. https://www.hinduamerican.org/blog/buddhist-mindfulness-is-all-the-rage-but-hinduism-has-a-deep-meditation-tradition-too

44. https://www.ncbi.nlm.nih.gov/pmc/articles/PMC6541086/

45. https://bibletalk.tv/what-other-religions-teach-about-salvation

46. https://en.wikipedia.org/wiki/Hinduism_and_Sikhism

47. https://www.learnreligions.com/highway-to-heaven-1770053

48. https://www.gotquestions.org/how-to-get-to-heaven.html

49. https://www.namb.net/apologetics/resource/mormon-plan-of-salvation/

50. https://www.pursuegod.org/what-mormons-believe-about-salvation/

51. https://en.wikipedia.org/wiki/Salvation

52. https://cs.mcgill.ca/~rwest/wikispeedia/wpcd/wp/s/Sikhism.htm

53. https://www.sikhismguide.net/heaven-after-life/

54. https://www.sikhsangat.com/index.php?/topic/18139-heaven-or-hell-according-to-sikhi/

55. https://www.wearesikhs.org/10_do_sikhs_believe_in_heaven_and_hell

56. https://www.sikhnet.com/news/concept-heaven-and-hell-gurbani

57. https://answersingenesis.org/jesus/jesus-is-god/10-biblical-reasons-jesus-is-god/

58. https://www.gotquestions.org/is-Jesus-God.html

59. https://www.npr.org/2014/04/07/300246095/if-jesus-never-called-himself-god-how-did-he-become-one

60. https://www.cru.org/us/en/how-to-know-god/is-jesus-god.html

61. https://www.britannica.com/biography/Jesus/The-picture-of-Christ-in-the-early-church-The-Apostles-Creed
62. https://www.npr.org/transcripts/300246095
63. https://kinginstitute.stanford.edu/king-papers/documents/humanity-and-divinity-jesus
64. https://www.michaeljkruger.com/did-the-earliest-christians-really-think-jesus-was-god-one-important-example/
65. https://www.shepherdaz.church/felt-needs/what-miracles-did-jesus-perform/
66. https://www.learnreligions.com/miracles-of-jesus-700158
67. https://www.christianity.com/wiki/jesus-christ/what-miracles-did-jesus-perform.html
68. https://bibilium.com/miracles-of-jesus-37-chronological-order/
69. https://liquidchurch.com/blogs/what-miracles-did-jesus-perform

CONCLUSION

As the author, I trust you enjoyed reading this book. I recognized from the outset that some readers might find some of the contents confronting, but I trust - not offensive.

This book challenges many of the engrained beliefs and teachings of some of the world's great religions. Here is a summary of some of the points made in the book's various chapters, followed by concluding comments.

The Divine: The author embraces the existence of the Divine. God has many names, and the terms used by different religions and belief systems can vary widely depending on cultural and historical contexts. Here are some examples of the names for God used by other faiths:

Christianity: Christians refer to God as "God," "Lord," "Father," "Almighty," "Savior," and "Creator," among other names. They believe in the Holy Trinity, consisting of God the Father, God the Son (Jesus Christ), and God the Holy Spirit.

Islam: Muslims refer to God as "Allah," which means "the God" in Arabic. Allah is considered the only God and is described as merciful, compassionate, and just.

Judaism: Jews refer to God as "Yahweh," "Adonai," "El," and "Elohim," among other names. They believe in one God who is omniscient, omnipotent, and omnipresent.

Hinduism: Hindus refer to God as "Brahman," "Vishnu," "Shiva," and "Krishna," among other names. They believe in a pantheon of gods and goddesses who are different manifestations of the one supreme being, Brahman.

Buddhists do not believe in a personal God but rather in a cosmic force called the "Dharma," which is the ultimate truth or reality that underlies all existence.

Sikhism: Sikhs refer to God as "Waheguru," which means "Wonderful Teacher" in Punjabi. They believe in one God who is omnipotent, omniscient, and compassionate. The names and concepts associated with God can be highly nuanced and complex and are often shaped by the historical and cultural contexts in which they arose.

Hell: According to the Christian (and other) faiths, Hell is an eternal place of punishment for sinners. It is not a physical place of torture but rather a spiritual one where the souls of the wicked are separated from God's presence and thus subject to torment and anguish. The Bible describes Hell as an "outer darkness" and a "lake of fire" where there will be "weeping and gnashing of teeth" (Matthew 8:12). It is a place of no hope, no mercy, and no escape. Christians are told that Hell is real and that those who have not accepted Jesus Christ as their Savior will spend eternity in this place of torment and despair. It is where God's wrath and justice are satisfied - those who have rejected God's love and mercy will experience. *(Ed. Scary stuff, so no wonder we were all terrified as children growing up).* However, the notion of being Heaven and Hell, as described in the Bible, may have been falsely represented or even perhaps invented; according to a distinguished Biblical Studies Professor Bart D, Ehrman who states *"... many of our ideas about heaven and hell emerged long after* Jesus's *time, through the struggle to explain the injustices of the world."* [14] (Bart D. Ehrman, 2020).

Proof : The scientific method's perspective on life after death is that it is currently impossible to prove or disprove its existence and that there is no evidence. The question of what happens after death remains one of the great mysteries of human existence and is a matter of personal belief and faith. This information reflects a widely held view among the scientific community, which is based on the current state of scientific understanding and the lack of empirical evidence for the existence of an afterlife or the soul beyond physical death. Despite the enormity of the question and your reflection on whether there is 'life after death,' it does not matter - the truth of the Mystery of Life will be revealed to each of us at our life-end. The author expresses the view that there is 'life after death' awaiting us all. This is also in alignment with the teachings of the afterlife in most major religions - with one major difference! Most, if not all, major religions pronounce their instructions as the 'only' way to find Heaven/Paradise/Nirvana in the afterlife; by definition, this means that if one does not follow the teaching of a particular brand of religion – they will not enter Heaven/Paradise/Nirvana.

Who gets to Heaven?

Each of the world's great religions is similar in its values, ethics, and morality, supported and promoted in their teachings to enter

233

Heaven/Paradise or Nirvana. These admirable values include being loving, caring, and compassionate to 'neighbors,' as well as other virtues consistent with the Golden Rule (refer to Chart 10.1 for an individual breakdown by faith).

However, each religion also has what this author calls *lynch-pin conditions*. This means that without obeying the parochial teaching of the religion's membership, one's entry into Heaven may not be actualized. These are the lynch-pin conditions by major religion:

For Christians to accept Jesus Christ as Savior, repent sins, and strive to live a life of obedience to God. To accept that Jesus is the embodiment of Father, Son, and Holy Ghost (see Trinity[1])

For Muslims to perform the pilgrimage to Mecca at least once in a lifetime. Fasting during the month of Ramadan and performing five daily prayers.

---

[1] The doctrine of the Christian Trinity emerged gradually over several centuries and was not developed by any single individual. The concept of the Trinity teaches that there is one God in three persons: the Father, the Son (Jesus Christ), and the Holy Spirit.

The earliest Christian writers, such as the apostles' Paul and John, recognized the divine nature of Jesus Christ and the Holy Spirit. Still, it wasn't until the fourth century that the doctrine of the Trinity was formally articulated.

One of the key figures in developing the doctrine of the Trinity was Athanasius, a theologian, and bishop of Alexandria in Egypt who lived in the fourth century. Athanasius defended the belief that Jesus Christ is fully divine and coequal with God the Father.

Another important figure in the development of the Trinity was the theologian Augustine of Hippo, who lived in the fifth century. Augustine emphasized the unity of the three persons in the Godhead and stressed the importance of the Holy Spirit as the bond of love between the Father and the Son.

It's important to note that the doctrine of the Trinity is not explicitly spelled out in the Bible but rather is a theological interpretation of biblical texts. The formalization of the doctrine of the Trinity was an attempt to explain and articulate the complex relationship between God the Father, Jesus Christ, and the Holy Spirit.

For Hindus to study the scriptures which contain the teachings of Hinduism.

For Buddhists to observe the Four Noble Truths.

For Sikhs to follow the Guru's teachings and instructions.

For Jews to observe the Torah. They are fulfilling other religious obligations. Observe the Sabbath and Jewish holidays.

The author respects all viewpoints and the right of individuals to their belief systems. However, the author proposes no 'winners' or 'losers' to enter the afterlife based on following the 'right' brand of faith or religion. It is suggested that all will be received equally, regardless of their religious following, including those without religion or knowledge of God. Purity of heart, quality of character, and compassion for others - will be a greater determinant than the parochial religious belief of who you 'arrived through.'

Respectfully, each major religion is self-serving by intimating that entering Heaven is via an exclusive pathway by following their teachings. Otherwise, sent to Hell for eternity, which is inconsistent with a loving and compassionate God.

The author suggests that God sees 'multiple truths,' and his ability far outweighs the comprehension of humankind. The value and contribution, and how he and she have lived their life, will be the greater determinant rather than which religion a person subscribed to.

Meaning and Purpose of Life

One might accrue wealth, fame, title, recognition, and power, but none will provide the joy, peace, and serenity sought. The meaning and purpose of life will not be achieved by looking egocentrically (inward at oneself) but exocentrically to help others less fortunate and those with greater needs than self. To find purpose and meaning in life, we each need to contribute to the life of others. To love your neighbor – not with platitudes but with actions. Life experiences in the natural world and the activities (good and bad) carry over to the spiritual world.

The Bible states, "...in my father's house, there are many mansions." [John 14 1-6]. This author contends there is no such absolute final place of Heaven or Hell in the afterlife but vertical levels (or planes) closer to God (the Light) and those distanced away from God (by definition, the darkness/evil).

The original meaning of the word 'mansion' was rooms. This suggests that the righteous and holy are the closest to God (Heaven) and those distanced away from God (of evil). Some researchers suggest there might be 8 to 9 different planes. Forgive the author's crude analogy, but it might better explain the concept - if one can picture a typical water basin faucet with two separate mixer taps – one for cold and the other for hot water. A user can adjust the taps to various running water temperatures by adjusting the two fixtures. Despite a variance of water temperature available (according to the level the taps are on), there is still a finite number of temperatures available. Boiling water is at one end of the range; at the other extreme, the water can be ambient cold. Maybe the planes between Heaven and Hell are akin to this analogy.

Distinguished Professor of Religious Studies at the University of North Carolina, Bart D. Ehrman, reports in his studies of ancient texts in his book "*Heaven and Hell - A History of the Afterlife*" some striking findings. These are paraphrased below and with thanks to Professor Ehrman for being allowed to share and cite the following:

"My scholarship led me to realize that the Bible was a very human book, with human mistakes, biases, and culturally conditioned views. And realizing that made me wonder if the beliefs in God and Christ I had held and urged on others were partially biased, culturally conditioned, or even mistaken". (Ehrman, 2020: xiv).

"I was hearing, and starting to think, that the Bible was not a consistent revelation whose very words came from God; that the traditional doctrines I had always held as obviously true (e.g., the Trinity) were not handed down from heaven but were formulations made by very fallible human beings; and that there were lots of other views out there – even Christian beliefs – that did not jibe with what I had long believed (Ehrman, loc cit, xv)."

"I'm (also) saying that the ideas of heaven and hell were invented and altered over the years. (Ehrman, loc cit, xvii).

Reincarnation.

This author cannot give an informed opinion as to whether reincarnation occurs. While there are significant reported cases that dedicated researchers have scientifically verified, the evidence remains anecdotal. Compared to the enormous body of anecdotal evidence of near-death experiences, which in the author's view provides compelling 'proof' of its existence, compared to reincarnation, which requires greater research and examination. However, while not knowing of the veracity of reincarnation, this author would not be surprised if this occurs and respectfully feels it makes perfect sense for God to assist the ongoing spiritual development of souls in the afterlife who may benefit from rebirth. By the Grace of God, all things are possible, and this might include reincarnation. Studies and research into past lives tend to support this possibility.

After fifty years of university research studies into NDE, there has been a major shift in belief and respect for the work undertaken by dedicated medical scientists, whose work in NDE was once considered pseudoscience to today's recognition of its veracity. The implication of positive findings on the legitimacy of NDEs is enormous as it provides a clearer scientific view of life after death.

Regarding grief and grieving, the author suggests one may never get over it (the loss), but with help, guidance, love, and support – there is the opportunity to get through it, which will take time. Living through the pain, albeit a minute at a time, then an hour at a time, progressing after that until the pain of the event softens. No magic or sacred words can be shared with someone grieving to remove the pain - just be there to provide comfort and support. There are good reasons to believe in an afterlife - those that hold this belief can often endure the suffering better, knowing that one day they will be in a loving reunion in the afterlife. The author strongly believes that 'the departed' are not 'gone' but remain close by - bound by love but in a different dimension.

There is no doubt there is a life after death and living in this physical (or natural) plane is part of the cycle of our preparation for the afterlife, and one's journey continues beyond the grave. The overwhelming evidence of near-death experiences adds testimony to this.

We are all on a pathway of learning and spiritual development. We take a legacy using what we have done to what we chose not to do.

Our loved ones who depart from us have not permanently left. They are certainly not (fully) in the cemetery awaiting decomposition (although their physical remains might be if they were buried). Their soul or spirit has long left their body and gone to the afterlife, greeted by loved ones waiting to welcome them. The ones who departed will also be a little sad to leave their living loved ones behind. However, they are often overwhelmed and delighted when they 'see and learn' the big picture. They now know that one day you will all be united.

Angels are messengers of God.

The word Angel originates from the Greek word "angelos," which means 'messenger.' The term was later adapted into Hebrew as "mal'kh," meaning "messenger'. Angels are messengers from Heaven, and there is ample evidence in the Holy Bible about devotees being visited (and spoken to by Angels). There is no reason not to believe that angels continue to see today but maybe not always visible. It is also reasonable that loved ones in spirit (as Angels) keep a watchful and loving eye on those remaining in the natural world to provide guidance and comfort where possible. They may also be undertaking their role as 'messengers,' and one needs to try and open and tune in to the message. When you have a strong sense or presence of a departed loved one or receive other signs, then there is a possibility they are nearer than you might think. This can be by sound (clearly hearing their voice calling out, audible to others), repeated lighting intensity changes (beyond faulty electricals), electronic devices turning on and off again, the strong fragrance of a loved one's perfume, visitations, and many other signs such as synchronicity. One-off happenings might be considered coincidental, but if repeated– you might be on to something!

I have observed countless times that within the first three to four weeks of passing, loved ones often try and let you know they are still around, albeit in spirit. They may converse with you when you are in deep sleep or when you have trained yourself in meditation to do so. I have personally experienced and reliably reported to me from people I know and trust many examples of communication, most are subtle, but other cases have been a lot more demonstrative, which is outside the scope of this book.

Your loved ones may also visit in your dreams or during quiet meditation. These abilities can be enriched and enhanced to aid greater psychic development.

If you want to share a message to or with a departed one, there is no real value or point in visiting the grave site as 'they' are not there, only their earthly remains. If you feel a strong presence from a loved one, they may already be around. Tune in to your senses, and do not dispel every incident as just being your imagination. These feelings and insights can be real.

Unsubstantiated but interesting reports from the research findings of Emanuel Swedenborg that in Heaven, spirits have a role to play and 'live' out times in a somewhat similar fashion to what they were able to in the natural world, according to their unique abilities and gifts.

Having a point of common agreement is good in a world of differing views. Suggestively, this point appears for the most part; the religions referred to in this book agree and support the existence of **Life After Death**. Christians refer to it as Heaven and Hell, Muslims as Paradise, and Buddhists Nirvana as the final goal. From this point onwards, each religion takes its parochial path for its devotees to reach Heaven/Paradise/Nirvana, as explained above.

It is suggested that every person on Earth has a purpose and value, as we have a soul or spirit with things to learn and teach. We all have life lessons to learn, and our time on this earthly plane is transitional until we enter the afterlife. However, what we do or fail to do in life has a carryover effect in the afterlife.

The author reserves his final view about what happens to a person's soul when someone intentionally takes their own life. Some religions purport these souls or spirits will go to an inescapable Hell. This author strongly believes this is fallacious, outrageous, and offensive to those beloved family members and friends left to grieve. A person who exits life in this way is like an 'actor' on the stage who, partway through the performance, takes an untimely stage exit and no longer continues with the performance, leaving scenes incomplete and dialogue left unspoken. The 'play' is left unfinished, with sets and acts no longer following as intended. The author believes any damaged soul will be lovingly received into Heaven and comforted accordingly. While the author doesn't know for certain, this is where reincarnation appears to make perfect sense but, of course, is subject to the Grace of God.

Everyone has a contribution, and we each have a role to play. The love, care, and compassion we show to others in this life, in helping the sick, the poor, the needy, and those suffering, is a way of discovering our meaning in life. Those who die being rich and famous will not be as memorable to those left behind as someone who showed love, care, compassion, and charity to others. In short, greater levels of happiness and purpose in this life will be found by doing for others what we would like done for us, given being in the same position. This aligns with the Golden Rule most of us grew up with: "Do unto others as you would do unto you." (A biblical principle in Luke 6:31 records Jesus saying, "Do to others as you would have them do to you." This statement is in the context of a lesson from Jesus about loving our enemies. Jesus took the conventional *quid pro quo* method of treating people and turned it on its head (see Matthew 5:38-48). Rather than doing to others what they have done to us or giving them what they may deserve, we are to treat them the way we want them to treat us.

241

Through free will, we can make choices; some might be 'good,' some may be 'bad,' while others could be horrendous, especially those that commit unspeakable crimes or harm others. We will each be accountable for our actions in passing, but the author does not support the myth of an absolute Heaven or Hell.

Being part of organized religion is a practical choice because it can foster all the important ingredients of good character, ethics, and values. Common sense based on a loving and compassionate God would not reasonably favor exclusive entry into Heaven as a reward for choosing the 'right' religion to follow. As an analogy to the words of Martin Luther King, Jr., where he pleads for black children of the future that "...one day they might be judged by the content of their character and not the color of their skin," lyrically applied, that entry into Heaven will be based on life lessons learned, the contribution made to humanity, help to the needy, compassion and love, and living a life of morality and honesty already reflected in the teachings of the world's great religions.

So, live a good life, follow a religion of your choice where you feel most comfortable, and be of service and kindness to others as part of the Natural Law and the Golden Rule. Your chosen religion (or none) can be your vehicle to reach Heaven, but it is not an 'express pass.'

We should all be respectful of each other's differing views and beliefs.

The author thanks you for reading this book, challenging as it may be. However, the author's objective has been served if reading Life After Death provides insight or stimulates reflection.

The author is happy to receive your blogs, or emails, on www.lifeafterdeath.au or email author@lifeafterdeath.au

Printed in Great Britain
by Amazon

45889705R00136